CW01669168

VIBRATIONS in LIFE'S MEMORY

Front and back covers: collage of life's memories

'Since wars begin in the minds of men, it is the minds of men that the defences of peace must be constructed.'

Unesco Constitution

VIBRATIONS
in
LIFE'S MEMORY

by

Dennis F.W. Hawes

ELSP

Published in 2005 by
ELSP
16A New St John's Road
St Helier
Jersey JE2 3LD

**All enquiries and correspondence regarding this book should be sent to its author, Dennis Hawes, at 2 Grace Taylor Mews
Folkestone, Kent, CT19 5UH**

Origination by Ex Libris Press, St Helier, Jersey
Typeset in 10/13.5 point Plantin
Headings in Trebuchet

Printed by Cromwell Press
Trowbridge
Wiltshire

ISBN 1 903341 97 3

Proceeds from the sale of this book will be donated to SSAFA – Soldiers, Sailors and Airforcemen's Association

CONTENTS

FAMILY

NATURE

SOCIETY

DEDICATION

This book is dedicated to the memory of my sister, Ivy, who, due to the miracle of our mutual wartime survival, remained so close to me and supported me all my life. Ivy shared my joys and sorrows, successes and failures, as I hope, I did hers. Her lifelong faith sustained not only her, but also me, until she passed away in 2003.

ACKNOWLEDGEMENTS

I am indebted to Ian Angus, a friend of very long standing, who persuaded me that my work was worth publishing, and without whom this book would not have come to fruition.

I would also like to thank my wife, Stella, whose editorial acumen and moral support were invaluable.

I am grateful to Charlotte Emmett for her excellent word-processing skills, and to the late Anna Brown, who gave me practical encouragement and advice.

Dennis Hawes
April 2005

INTRODUCTION

To give retrospective, creative expression to the extreme experiences of our lives is recognised as a healing process. When that expression is the written word, there is another dimension: the readers are given a privileged opportunity to gain a glimpse into those experiences.

In this book, we journey with the author from the island of Malta to the Kentish North Downs, via war-stricken Europe, exploring the gamut of life stories en route. Surely Thomas Carlyle's maxim would apply to this volume: 'If a book comes from the heart, it will contrive to reach other hearts'.

I am proud to commend Dennis' book to you. May it inspire us all to rise with hope and faith from the fires of our own traumas, to where the phoenix flies in peace.

Stella Hawes

Dennis in Ivy's nursery just after World War II

Safe harbour: Folkestone fishing boats, Christmas 1989

ABOUT THE AUTHOR

Dennis Hawes was born in 1923, in Malta, to Frank and Daisy Hawes, and was the youngest of four children. Frank had remained in the army after the First World War. It was a close-knit, loving family. Sadly, Frank died in 1930 and the parents being Londoners, Daisy brought the children to London to be near relations. Dennis' elder brother Eric, had enlisted in the army at 14 and Ivy, the elder sister, went into service. Eve and Dennis remained with their mother. This was the time of the great depression and their personal poverty, and that of many working people, was something they never forgot.

Dennis went to an LCC Central Technical School, leaving in 1939 with the Oxford School Certificate. Eric imparted very left wing views to Ivy and Dennis; he subscribed to Left Book Club, which all the family read except Eve. The family fortunes improved and Ivy returned home. Eve and Dennis started work and the family acquired a modern flat near Mornington Crescent, London NW1. Tragically, this was demolished by a parachute mine in 1941. Eve and Daisy were killed and Dennis rescued Ivy from the rubble. Dennis was working in the St Pancras (Camden) public library at the time.

The author went into the army and served four years in the infantry, taking part in three assault landings: Sicily, Italy and Normandy. He transferred to the Royal Army Education Corps in Germany in 1945. He became Command Librarian 1st Corps in 1946. In 1945, Eric was killed in Burma.

Dennis returned to the UK and worked for three public library authorities, St Pancras, Paddington and Finsbury, all subsumed into larger authorities in the mid 1960s. He studied part-time to obtain his Associateship and Fellowship of the Library Association at North Western Polytechnic, London. Later, he gained an MA at University College, London. In 1961 he became Librarian of the Borough Polytechnic and eventually Head of Library Services and Educational Technology at Polytechnic of the South Bank. Dennis was elected a member of the Royal Society of Arts in 1973.

He managed the introduction of the GEAC automation programme in 1983, which, with Hull University, was the most advanced on-line system in the UK. He was joint author of 'Library Automation at the South Bank 1983.' He served on the governing body of the Polytechnic and was elected a Fellow in 1985 on his retirement, when he moved to Folkestone, Kent.

He joined the Shepway Writers, a local group and wrote a considerable amount of poetry and prose. Dennis also took art classes and, having studied calligraphy before retirement, taught this subject for two years. He became a swimming coach for Folkestone Swimming Club for ten years, taking the Amateur Swimming Association Teacher's Certificate. He was also a primary school governor for a few years. As an ex-Londoner, Dennis loved to walk in the local countryside with friends. He was diagnosed with cancer of the prostate in 1994 and given a maximum of three years to live – new drugs have given remission.

Dennis has wide reading interests: fiction, poetry, history, politics, history of science and technical education. His radical politics have always stayed with him. Dennis is a committed Christian, belonging to an evangelical Anglican church and likes to go to Canterbury Cathedral occasionally. He enjoys going to classical concerts with his wife whenever possible and is regularly exercised by his dog.

Acronyms

MO	Medical officer
RAP	Regimental Aid Post
88	Multi-purpose high velocity German gun
Sgt.	Sergeant
RAMC	Royal Army Medical Corps
LCT	Landing Craft Tank
LCA	Landing Craft Assault
50th	50th Infantry Division
PBI	"Poor Bloody Infantry" (WW1 slang)
NCO	Non-commissioned officer (Corporal, Sergeant, Sergeant-Major)
RASC	Royal Army Service Corps
MM	Military Medal
CSM	Company Sergeant-Major
POW	Prisoner of War
QM	Quarter master
HQ	Headquarters
ARP	Air Raid Precautions
CO	Commanding Officer
DLI	Durham Light Infantry
MC	Military Cross
PIAT	Projectile Infantry Anti Tank
AA	Anti Aircraft
SP	Self-propelled gun

Left: My brother Eric on leave from West Africa before going to Burma, September 1943

Above: My sisters Eve (left) and Ivy, 1940. Eve was killed with my mother in an air raid, 19 March 1940

Left: Nobby (left) and Dennis before D-Day, April 1944

Right: Platoon of Hampshires in Arromanches, 6 June 1944

19th March 1941

It had been a quiet, starlit night.
The bombing and Ack-Ack fire light.
Not like the heavy raids that
Lit up the London night for days,
With a fiery, pulsating glow over the skyline
Threatening life, limb and sanity.

In our flat the radiogram was playing softly.
My mother and sisters were anxious but lively.
Restless, I left for fresh air.
I paused under an archway and heard
The sinister throb of an aircraft overhead,
Waited for the roar of the bombs,
But there was just an eerie silence.

Then suddenly an eye-searing white flash,
A deafening explosion,
A rush of hot wind,
Which plucked my feet from under me.
Then a cloud of acrid, fume-laden dust
Rolled over me, as I realised
It had been a parachute mine,
Which had floated down silently in the darkness.

Shakily, I stood up, crunched and slithered
Across the shattered masonry and splintered glass,
To where our flat had been.
The pale stars shone through
The roofless building.

Their light picked out the gaunt, ruined walls
The piles of bricks, girders, fractured concrete.
In a corner a broken water pipe
Spurted a stream of water over the debris.
There was no sign of life in the desolation.

Then under a mound of rubble
Where the kitchen once had been,
Came a scrabbling sound and slowly
Appeared the bleeding head of my sister Ivy.
We heaved together and as by a miracle,
She struggled free: cut, bruised but whole.
We clung together, tried to take in the loss,
With conflicting emotions of grief and relief,
Of my mother and sister's violent death
And our mysterious survival.

The bombers came back again in that same night
Spreading destruction, pain, death, and fright.
But who can say why some are spared and others lost?
For only Thou, Oh Lord, will know the ultimate cost.

66 Datchet House, London NW. March 1941

BEATING THE SYSTEM

It is a clever soldier that can put one over on the army, which usually has the last word. Once, I thought I had brought off the perfect coup. I leave you my reader to judge.

In 1942 I was serving in a holding battalion on the Norfolk coast from which drafts were regularly sent overseas. Here I was being trained as a signaller and enjoyed the instruction. My previous training had been foot drill, route marches, some assault courses, twice on the range and a kind of battle drill carried out on the Barrack square. The latter being not only farcical but misleadingly dangerous. It also included such gems as 'Fixing bayonets by numbers' and 'As for delivering a message to the front, salute.' Bullshit was supposed to be abolished after the Dunkirk disaster, but soon crept back into the army system. The nation that had pioneered the tank and aircraft cooperation with artillery and infantry seemed to be back to 1913. To send a force in 1940 to France, consisting of 12 infantry divisions and just two armoured brigades, showed how little had been learned from the battles of 1918. It took nearly three years after Dunkirk to develop some serious cooperation between armour, aircraft, artillery and infantry. Even so, it never reached the standard of the Germans, even by 1945. Infantry tactics were badly taught and infantry weapons inferior to those of the enemy in WW2.

To return to Norfolk, the particular bete noir, or perhaps the bete rouge, of our company was called Powell, a red-faced choleric Scot. In addition to the usual quota of drill, this CSM imposed an extra half hour of foot drill before breakfast, called Sandy's half hour, after a famous cinema organist of the period. The parade was held in the dawn light, but this would not preclude a rigorous inspection, usually yielding a sprinkling of prospective janker wallahs. Two men who had imprudently shaved each other's necks to evade the regulation scalping, were made to stand in front of the company, while he shouted abuse at them calling them queers and poofs. They were then promptly marched off to the guardroom. Most of the training seemed to be left to the NCO's, officers were rarely seen at this time.

Autumn drifted into winter and in addition to our guard duties on the coast defences, we were sent out to pull sugar beets in the wet, frozen fields. The work was hard; the beets were pulled up by hand, topped and tailed with a sickle. This was field conditions. Of course the army boots could not keep out the wet and as boots were polished by this unit, not dubbined as decreed after Dunkirk, getting cleaned up for guard duty was difficult.

Came the inevitable day when we received orders to go overseas. Vast quantities of kit were issued to us that filled two kit bags. My USA WW1 rifle was exchanged for a British WW1 one and we had various injections. In three months time I would be sent to the front with a small pack and all the other kit handed back to the QM, less the few things that could be crammed into a larger pack. The night before departure, we had as fair a booze up as our 14s a week, (less deductions for leave and barrack room damages) would allow, then went back to the billets. This was a run-down hotel, with unheated rooms, cold-water washing, no baths or showers, latrine facilities for crapping in the backyard. A concession had been made for night calls and a large iron bucket placed on the landing. The night of our departure it was nearly full to the top.

Our sleep was brief; we slept in our uniforms and were roused at 3.30 am. It was then, in a blinding flash, I realised that with the company office directly underneath, I was ideally placed for my master stroke. I waited until the last man had clattered down the rickety stairs and pulled the great iron bucket over. The noxious urine foamed in a yellow flood as it poured down the stairs and spread over the landing above the company office. I followed behind, being careful to avoid being splashed unduly.

We paraded in the yard outside the Hotel. I took care to stand in the rear rank, wondering if I could suppress my laughter. Soon Sandy came out. In the dim light, little could be seen but one could almost feel the vibrations of rage and frustration, as he danced up and down in fury. Everything he said increased our enjoyment. All his vain bluster about court martials, detention, calling in the MP's, tracking us to our next unit, merely stoked our inner laughter and pleasure. Finally he spoke of the damage to the company office, how the piss had doused out the lights and the foul mess someone would pay for. We all knew he could do nothing but shout and bluster. We all got on the trucks shaking and weeping with suppressed joy. Hours later on the train to the port, we were still chuckling. Only the horrors of the troop ship, with two months of incredible discomfort round the Cape, silenced us.

When we arrived in Egypt we were posted to an experienced battalion and received the kind of training which was so absent from that in the UK, and getting to see and know our officers on a daily basis. Cheering myself up when we got on the assault boat for the Sicily landing, I said to a friend "Do you remember old Sandy?" He replied, "Well he got the last laugh, he's certainly still in England, and anyway some other poor sods would have to clear up the mess."

GREATER LOVE

They dropped us into the squally sea, that dark night.
The waves flung us back against the ship's hull.
We spent the hours of darkness bailing out
The sea that came over the sides of the craft,
Which left most of the men retching, in two feet of water,
Death an acceptable option.

From the unseen shoreline, the
Red, green and yellow tracer which
Beckoned and taunted the invasion force.
The night sky was illuminated by flares
And the flash of exploding bombs dropped by the RAF.

Towards dawn, the wind and the waves dropped
And we came in on a glassy sea, in bright sunshine,
With shells splashing nearby, hitting another craft,
Which exploded with startling, orange violence.
We splashed ashore near the small port,
Gardens and vineyards seemed verdant after the desert.
Vivid the bright scarlet of the wounded, tended
In the yard of a fisherman's cottage.
Crumpled, green, ragged, Italian dead in a ditch.
Black, dirty, exploding shells in the dazzling light.

Then you fired on us with a light machine gun,
From a vineyard and fled.
We pursued you, when you ran into the farmhouse.
We waited, sweating, panting, for your next move.
Suddenly you ran out, 15 assorted weapons fired.

You went down and then the doors were flung open –
Disgorging a horde of hysterical Sicilian families,
Gesticulating, screaming, crying and shouting.

We carried you into the farmhouse,
You had only one wound, but we had orders,
"To shoot all prisoners in the first phase."
I looked at your handsome face and open brown eyes,
The dark hole, welling blood from your groin.
It was an order, to be ignored.
Then the stretcher-bearers came and took you away.

You showed great courage, in coming from
That farmhouse to almost certain death.
Ready to lay down your life, for those families.
You could never have guessed, that the Lord was on
Your side, together with our poor marksmanship.

Marzemimi, Pachino, Sicily 1943

THE REINFORCEMENT

The baked, purple-black hills
Roasted under the brazen sun
Which gripped the plateau, in a furnace vice.

Then the sky darkened under the menacing clouds,
Thunder and lightening rumbled and crackled
Around the enclosed rocks and scrub.
Then a blessed downpour of rain,
Soaked our stinking, dirty khaki drill.
Our faces turned up, licking in the heavy drops.
The storm passed and the sun scorched us again,
Drying us swiftly, as if the rain
Had never been.

We shook out in extended order,
Moving cautiously through the olive groves
On each side of the road.
As the ground rose near the farmhouse,
A hail of machine gun fire came
Screeching towards us,
Cutting off the tops of the long grass,
Shredding the cactus and
Ricocheting off the stone walls and boulders.

Cowering, crushed into the dry soil we waited,
Almost beyond any expectation of survival.
Then we heard the crack of our tank's gun
Which fired behind us.
The ragged cheer of our men

On the other side of the road,
The chatter and thud of tommy guns and grenades.

Shakily we rose to look at the prisoners,
But you, the reinforcement, did not get up.
They turned you over to look at your wounds,
The hole in your back that silenced your heart,
A rare clean death with one small hole.

You came into the line last night.
We didn't have time to learn your name,
Although it was dear to someone.
So we had to look at your paybook,
To report your sacrifice for King and country.

Agira, Sicily 1943

THEY ALSO SERVE

Dear old Len, you never resented being a batman,
Looked after your officer with gentle affection.
Efficient in our quiet countryman's way.
He'll miss you, nobody wants your job now.

We were all scared, when they shelled us,
Moving up the mountain road, in those lorries.
Blazing vehicles lighting up the purpling sky.
You were calm as we moved into the olive grove.
Said nothing as we deployed in the dusk
Under the stone wall and cactus bushes.
You got down just in front of me,
Your hob nailed boots close to my face.

Then came the shuttering whine of a shell,
The special sound which tells you its close.
It burst on your sturdy fair body,
Blew you to bits, strewing your limbs,
Before me, beside me and upon me.

Dirty, deafened, shaking, slightly wounded,
I crouched and saw the bloody shambles
Once forming your body and encasing your soul.
I limped away to the Regimental Aid Post,
The memory of your bloody, violent end,
To carry with me for a lifetime.

The company captured thousands of lira that night,
Letting it blow around the hillside,

Believing only the army currency was valid,
Only to be paid out with the Italian money
On their first spell, out of the line.

But why did you draw so much of that army currency,
That was scattered over your crimson, serpentine guts:
You were the least money-conscious of men.
Where did you hope to spent it
In this desolate, furnace of the Sicilian hills?

It could only have been for your wife and kids.
You didn't gamble, smoke or drink,
Except for a pint of ale in the village pub.

How long will they remember you in the Public Bar?

River Dittaino, Sicily 1943

WHAT WILL THEY TELL THE FOLKS BACK HOME?

We came through the small wood in the valley,
Skirting the bomb craters as we emerged,
A single 88 was firing over our heads,
At a hill behind us, where a lorry blazed.
We dug in behind a rise, topped by a farmhouse.
The first ranging shots came over quickly.
Frantically we scraped and dug between shell bursts,
Then lay in the deepened holes, their sides quaking
With near misses and fragments twittering across
Our slit trenches, often embedded in the spoil.

So it continued, intermittently most of the day.
Then towards evening another company came
Through our lines to attack.
The shells and Nebelwerfers intensified,
As they moved forward, it seemed a miracle
So many had survived as they came past our holes,
In the gathering gloom,
Grim faced, but some with a bitter joke to crack.
The attack was not pressed home
And they fell back to run the gauntlet of fire again.

Then followed a lull in the firing.
It was then no doubt, with your bladder or bowels
An urgent problem, you decided to relieve yourself.
Why did you choose to go forward,
Instead of to the rear of our positions?

As you came back we all heard the challenge of the sentry,

Unanswered by you and then the crack of a rifle.
The agonised cry of "Oh you've shot me".
Will never be forgotten by those who heard it.

We carried you into the farmhouse,
Then the shells and mortars started again,
They blew in the windows and shutters
As we dressed the ugly wound in your stomach.

It was some time before they got an ambulance
Up the twisting mountain road.
We never found out, if you lived or died
And what they told the folks back home.
Was it wounded or killed in action?

Before Regalbuto, Sicily 1943

DUST TO DUST

We ran through the night barrage,
Deafened, blinded, shaken,
Lying down, at times clasped together,
As if to cheat a solitary death.
Then after hours of relentless noise and terror.
All became mysteriously still.

As we guided the ambulance up the track,
I saw you,
Patinated by the glow of the full moon,
Overlaid with white dust,
You lay as if carved in marble,
Against the darkened olive grove.

Although you had lost a leg,
Yet you were beautiful in death,
Like some broken Greek masterpiece
Merged now into this ancient landscape,
Which has witnessed so many bloody conflicts.

Transcended now from the fear of hovering death,
Waiting to strike, at any time, by day or night.
The hideous noise of exploding shells and mortars,
Searching fire of rasping machine guns or snipers.
Smells of sweat, dirt, fear, fresh blood or decaying
Corpses, mixed with the aromatic herbs and pine scent.
No more tongue-swollen thirst in the furnace heat,
Fearing your courage will be drained by anxiety and fatigue.

But now those black, forbidding ridges,
Which malevolently watched our every move,
Seem softened now, in the velvet darkness,
Even tranquil in the balmy night.
So I pray my dear, unknown, broken friend,
That peace has come to you
And all who fell this day.

Before Regalbuto, Sicily 1942

THE LAST RIDGE

At the first light of the brassy dawn,
Its rays fingering the baked, black, barren hills,
Came the crack of a sniper's rifle.
Then heavy, stumbling footsteps,
Crashing, tumbling, writhing body,
Of the company Sergeant Major.

Eyes gazing into mine wordlessly,
Staring, bulbous, terror-stricken,
Inhuman sounds of grunting and moaning,
Word dumb like a stricken beast.
Dark, jagged, crimson crater in your throat,
Spurting jet of bright red,
Drenching my thin Italian blanket,
Spraying and staining the spoil of my trench.
Thick, cloying smell of viscous, arterial blood.

Face turning from brick red to grey green.
No use the thick, shell dressings,
Soon, soaked, soggy, saturated red cloths,
Bravely applied by scared stretcher bearers.
Your wound so gaping, terrible, terminal,
Hopeless even in the hands of a skilled surgeon.

What were you doing so carelessly on that ghastly ridge?
Where so many had died, friend and foe together,
Intermingled, intertwined, in grotesque comradeship,
Each offering a personal posture, to the rising sun.
The same, but differing as death chose you.

Black, bloated, green, gaseous, crumpled bundles.
Some so thinly buried near our holes, they
Stiffen and reach out to us, through the meagre soil.

All around, the shattered, shell-shorn, splintered olive trees,
The cactus shredded to lace, the pock-marked terraces.
Man with the ravaged landscape, in a shared calvary.
You are one with those fallen, in this furnace of hell.
May God have mercy on you and those who lie on this ridge
And pity on us, who go on to face another awesome dawn.

Regalbuto Ridge, Sicily 1943

ITALY, SEPTEMBER 1943

There was a moment in history when I may well have been among the most forward soldiers of the Allied armies in Europe. Our battalion, the 1st Hampshires, had taken part in the invasion of Sicily and the subsequent campaign. When the fighting was over we were billeted in a village called Piedmonte at the foot of the then quiescent Etna volcano. Here we had our filthy clothes washed by the village women, only after they had been calmed down, after trying to storm the Regimental Aid Post for food. We went down to swim in the sapphire sea, at that time clean and unpolluted, and gazed at the Italian shoreline, across the Straits of Messina. We also slept a great deal, to make up for the continual loss of sleep one has to accept in the front line.

One day a party of us drove out in an armoured car (used as an ambulance) to look for a wine cellar, which, we had been told was situated in a deserted farmhouse, used as a German dressing station. There were several graves in the farmyard, also scraps of bloody crepe paper lying around, which the Germans had used as bandages. We went into the cellar, which was several inches deep in red wine which had leaked from the barrels. We filled up a very large, wicker-covered demi-john from one of the undamaged casks. Alas, when we started to return, the soft black volcanic soil gave way under the vehicle and we ended up sitting upside down but uninjured. Luckily the wine was intact! I believe the driver spent a scary night at the farmhouse, waiting for the recovery unit.

Inevitably, it was announced that we would be invading Italy. The briefing took place in an olive grove, to the background of a signals truck softly transmitting 'Tuxedo Junction', a popular Glen Miller number of the period. As I had been a keen dancer the year before enlistment, I found myself humming and jiving at the back, with scant regard for the briefing. The plan was that two of our rifle companies, plus a Royal Marine Commando would lead the assault, followed by the rest of the unit later. It was hoped this venture would distract the Germans from the main allied invasion, further north up the coast at Salerno. This was the furthest distance the Air forces said they could provide cover.

After the briefing I went with a small group from my platoon to purchase a goat as a change from tinned food and hard biscuits. A better description would be to describe the transaction as theft, given the few tins of corned beef offered to the peasant in exchange, despite his protest. One of the group, borrowing an officer's pistol, shot the goat and then gave a virtuoso performance of butchery on the hoof, with a bayonet and clasp knife. The hide was peeled off, head removed, then it was disembowelled, cut into joints and soon broiling in old cut-down petrol tins with some looted fresh vegetables. The cooling stew was eaten in the hold of the LCI (a craft designed to land follow-up troops) en route to Italy. The previous evening, before the invasion, we had all slept on the beach overlooking the Straits of Messina, in whose sapphire, clear sea we had often bathed. Then a thunderstorm broke which drenched practically everybody, except myself sleeping under a stretcher dug in the sand. Next morning the sands were filled with cursing soldiery trying to get dry in the hot sun. Perhaps I should say I had recently volunteered to be a stretcher-bearer from being a rifleman. My motives were mixed, from getting out of patrols to genuine interest in the job. Some brief training plus boy scouts and ARP experience sufficed, but I soon discovered I was out of the frying pan into the fire, literally, as often we had to get out of our slits while others stayed put.

I must have dropped off on the LCI, because I woke to the sound of the ship's keel grounding on the sand. We filed down the gangway and on to the shore where some buildings were still smouldering. Now we could hear the Germans shelling the beach north of us, which should have been empty. We marched along the lower coast road and climbed up to attack the higher coast road, where the leading platoon of our company attacked some German transport. The crack of grenades and small arms fire could be heard. I went forward with my fellow stretcher bearer, Sandy, and me were soon dressing some German wounded while other prisoners were escorted to the rear, carrying those who needed it.

It was by then light and we could see the main invasion fleet making its way ashore in daylight. Cleary something had gone wrong and it transpired that the navy had lost the first assault wave. One of these incoming craft, a flak boat, decided we were Germans and drenched our positions with light AA fire. Not the first or last time of friendly fire. Soon myriad explosions spouted from the rocks and terraces, miraculously only one soldier was killed and one wounded. We carried the wounded one into a small hut, of which the door and windows were missing. The hut overlooked the bay. No sooner had the boat's fire stopped than we were bombed and strafed by an American fighter. The Germans, always great opportunists in battle, then chose to counterattack and I later thought they had been reinforced by infantry. They came down the slope, firing all their weapons at random as was their tactic, bearing in mind they had far faster firing automatic weapons than we had, and were also covered by mortar fire. Soon the air was filled with scores of bullets buzzing like angry hornets, much of it aimed to intimidate the opposition. They succeeded in this and our company fell back down the slope, one lone Bren gunner firing from the door of the hut and then jumping out of the window.

This left us with a screaming, wounded man, with a piece of shrapnel from the flak boat lodged in his ankle. We hastily stuffed our grimy handkerchiefs in his mouth to gag him and just waited. The sound of German voices could be heard plainly and the chink of their equipment on the terraces. We waited silently, the wounded man also fell silent, understanding the situation. Through the opening of the door-less entrance we could see the soles of the hobnailed boots of a dead comrade. What next, a grenade? A burst of automatic fire, or at best, prisoners? Then the German voices receded up the slope and we heaved a sigh of relief. Soon the German machine guns opened up, a short way further up the slope with the screeching, ripping sound they made with their high rate of fire. They would fire for most of the day and part of the night, lighting up the hut with their flashes. We could hear the harsh instructions to their mortars and the plop of the bomb as it hit the end of the tube before whistling overhead.

Out in the bay the main invasion fleet moved slowly to the shore. The Germans were obviously now reinforced by tanks or assault guns. A few German planes started to appear, to bomb and strafe the ships, now under serious artillery fire from the German positions. In addition, some of the transport on their decks caught fire. Further out to sea, a British monitor started to shell the enemy positions, some of which were entrenched in a nearby cemetery. The 15-inch shells were coming close to the hut, which was already in the centre of fire and counter-fire, as the British artillery was landed. I couldn't resist peeping out of the window to watch the panorama of the invasion and seeing a patrol of commandos attempting to move along the coast road. They didn't get far, as the Germans occupied the high ground and could see every move. It was the same tactical story as in Sicily and would continue the length of Italy, with the enemy always being in the best defensive positions.

During the day, the wounded man wanted to defecate and urinate and his mess tins were made available. We drank our water sparingly although it was scorching hot in the small hut. At one time, peeping out of the window and looking at the azure blue skies, the sapphire sea, the cypresses, laden vineyards and the coloured cottages, I said to myself: "Not a bad place to die," as I truly expected to do. Later, when I read "Now more than ever seems it rich to die," written by John Keats, I thought I understood the line somewhat better.

The interminable day of fire and counter-fire left us cowering in the corner of the hut as yet more tiles slid from the roof. The long hours of the day seemed as if they would never end.

Fortunately, it was September and not June and at sunset, after a spectacular display or orange and purple over the sky and sea, the fire slackened. The German machine guns still lit up our hut at intervals as well as the sound of their mortar commands. At dusk I slipped out of the hut to fill our water bottles from a small pipe which came from a spring into a stone basin just outside, fear and anxiety increased our thirst, of course. At about 3.00am we heard the sound of tracked and wheeled vehicles moving off. Later, we heard the main allied invasion had gone in at Salerno.

Just after dawn, with another amazing sunrise, we carried the wounded man down the slope to the lower coast road. Half way down, I paused to cram some ripe black grapes into my mouth – they were covered with morning dew. It was a sensation I shall never forget. We met a British patrol on the lower road, and came back to HQ to be debriefed. Breakfast was fatty cold bacon and ration biscuits but it was the tea they gave us which was like nectar. Two hours after our return, we all started to march along the upper coast road, to try and catch up with the Germans. We marched all that day and into the following night until about 3.00am, halting only to let the engineers clear the mines. The German rear guard struck back only once with an armoured car which wounded the brigadier, (Urquhart) and killed his driver. Eventually we halted in a dry water course where we were expected to dig in. A few shallow holes were made into which we collapsed, after almost three sleepless nights. Of course, there had been no food except the ration biscuits which many prudent soldiers carried in their packs. Our water bottles had been filled when we started.

After two weeks, the Brigade went back to Sicily, minus the recent reinforcements – so much for the regimental system in wartime. On the troop ship going back to the UK, the C.O., at a large meeting, informed us we were going back to England for the invasion of Europe. For many of the battalion, this would be their first home leave for 7-10 years. The inhumanity of such a period abroad must, today, seem incredible. Of course, the next invasion was Normandy, a landing on a much larger scale with the Germans fielding the largest and best equipped army which the Western Allies had encountered during WW2.

Being part of history can sometimes have its hazards!

CARRY ME BACK TO BLIGHTY

October can be golden, glorious in Sicily.
We camped in the open, just outside Syracuse,
The fighting over at least for a while
Just a few parades and fatigues.
Plenty of good food, water and tea.
Hours of lost sleep regained under the
Olive trees by day, and the stars by night,
Swimming in the clear sapphire waters
Under a warm, blue cloudless sky.
Concerts in the Greek amphitheatre,
Where Gracie Fields is barracked by
A handful of jingoists.

Then they dumped some crumpled battledresses,
Into the corner of a field.
We're going back to Blighty
For the invasion of Europe, they said.
Who cares, we'll be out of the line
And we'll see our families and friends.
Not to worry about the invasion.
In a few months hence, the war could be over
The RAF and the Russians might finish it off.

You must have known you were really sick,
When that bout of Malaria hit you,
But you were terrified of missing the boat,
Staying behind, being sent back to the front.

I saw your face, as we got on the lighters,
To be ferried out to the troopship,
It was purple-green under the tan.
You still didn't go sick on the boat.
"It'll go when the boat sails," you said.

But when the boat sailed, you were ashore.
Dead with cerebral malaria.
So they buried you in the Military cemetery,
At Catania, together with the others
Who fell during the campaign.

Syracuse, Sicily 1943

D-DAY JUNE 6th, 1944

The dawn made a struggling appearance for a June day. Dark skies and scudding clouds cast a reluctant light over the squally, slate-coloured sea. As the light improved, the plunging shapes of the vast invasion fleet loomed out of the darkness. The heavy swell was breaking over the bows of the smaller vessels. Shells from the larger battleships had been passing over in the darkness and aircraft had been heard overhead most of the night. As we drew nearer to the shore the smaller boats and rocket ships started to drench the beaches.

Gradually, ahead, the low line of the sand and the sea wall came into focus. Behind were the green fields, but the buildings had a somewhat unfamiliar look. The landscape was almost like our own coast, but not quite. It had just that sinister distortion of reality which is often present in bad dreams. Then what else is a battle to most people, but a nightmare? How we all wanted to get back on dry land, but we knew the final stretch of sea was the most dangerous. Then there would be the unknown terror that awaited us at the shoreline, as we struggled ashore when the ramp went down. Finally we knew that, after the beach defences, there would be the campaign to face.

There had been little sea sickness on our boat, but then we had been 'messing about in boats', training for months. Moreover this was our third assault landing. There were, however, some new men in the battalion, who came as reinforcements. Perhaps our apparent coolness had, in fact, an element of fatalism brought about by previous experiences. At all events, whatever the anxieties, there could be no question of retreat. Where could anyone retreat to? Sadly, many survivors of the Mediterranean campaigns would end their soldiering on the beaches or fields of Normandy.

The shoreline had long since broken its foreboding silence, as the shell bursts which erupted along its surface were returned by the shore batteries. Menacing fingers formed from pillars of black smoke beckoned us to the boiling foreshore. Large battles can sometimes generate their own fiery momentum but it is often the long slogging campaigns that test the endurance of the infantry.

The final objective for our battalion, the 1st Hampshire, was the town of Arromanches and the hills of Tracy behind it. We were to land at Le Hamel, Asnelles, then swing south to roll up the shore defences. It all looked daunting, even on the excellent briefing. But we all knew at this stage of the war, that it is a rare battle, which goes according to plan. Two of the rifle companies were to lead the assault, covered by amphibious armour and flail tanks to destroy the mines. These would be quickly followed by the two other reserve companies, passing through them to the next objective. Battalion headquarters would then go in forty-five minutes later, with signals, adjutant, regimental aid post etc. For this invasion I was detailed to land with the Battalion HQ. On previous landings, I had been with the rifle companies. I didn't need anyone to tell me how lucky I was this time. The medical Sergeant, with three stretcher bearers (including myself) were to set up an aid post just off the beach. This was optimistically marked on the battle map. The M | O had decided to go in with the second wave. We were carrying large packs crammed with medical supplies, in addition to our normal equipment.

The crossing from Lymington on an LCT (landing Craft Tank) had been unpleasant but uneventful. There was no attempt to sleep on the cold deck and no accommodation except for the crew. The early morning light had, however, revealed a somewhat bizarre and forlorn figure. Gazing miserably into the heavy swell was a soldier wearing a coloured walking-out cap and civvy shoes. His equipment was comprised of a cheap fibre case. This deserter, caught just before we embarked, may not have been the oddest person making for the French coast, but was among the most useless. The adjutant's decision, repeated by all who heard to the others, "*If we go, so do you*" may now seem stupid, but at the time produced grim chuckles of amusement. This deserter some how got back to England, but was killed by a V.I. flying bomb.

As the LCT drew inshore, we were ordered to climb on the tanks and other armoured vehicles to disembark. At that time two light shells hit the bridge and a shower of splinters descended upon us. The sense of exposure and vulnerability on that choppy sea was unpleasant. Nevertheless we were cheered by the sight of an armoured bulldozer, ploughing its way through the waves. Unfortunately, the Churchill tank to which we were clinging became waterlogged after trundling a few yards. There was some panic as the incoming tide and heavy seas broke over the troops trying to keep a grip on the slippery hull of the tank. Then another salvo of shells splashed in the water around us, one hitting the LCT, which pulled out of sea.

What happened next, I cannot say for sure. I slipped off my already loose equipment, which sank to join the vast collection of militaria deposited on the seabed that day and which they were still fishing out forty years later. I was sure that with the inflated lifebelt, I could swim the few hundred yards to the shore. Two or three others joined me in this cold swim of the last stretch of the channel. I found out later that the Sergeant was wounded and the other two medics were drowned. I have felt badly about this ever since, as I made no attempt to help them. Everyman for himself? On the 40th anniversary I searched for their grave, in all the beachhead cemeteries, but did not find them. They must have been lost in the sea.

After struggling in the sea some distance, we were picked up by a fire support craft, which drew away from the shore. We lay cold and breathless on the narrow deck. Our rest was brief and when an LCA (Landing Craft Assault) came across our bows, we were transferred into its stern. "If we go, so do you". The LCA contained a platoon of the Green Howards, part of our division but headed for another sector of the beach. Shivering and soaked we cowered in the stern as it ploughed ahead, sea and spray coming over the bows. Some tea laced with rum was offered to me, the smell of the liquor made me queasy so I declined.

As we came nearer to the shore we took a quick look at the burning wreckage on the beach and close by a boat blew up on one of the mined obstacles. I take it this was why the coxswain lost his nerve and refused to take us in. There was a heated exchange between the platoon officer and skipper. The officer hailed a withdrawing craft into which we clambered. This would have been a disaster, if the platoon had not been a follow-up group. The less nervy coxswain steered us skilfully through the deadly stakes with their mines and fused shells, to shore. Not quite, as the water was waist deep as we disembarked. Looking back over my shoulder, I saw another incoming craft explode on a beach obstacle. With a mighty orange flash, it was flung into the air, to settle with a crash and cascade of debris, partly human.

The 'Howards' then made off in truly veteran style, despite the harassing gunfire. In the short time we were with them few words had been spoken. They knew what they had to do, and in their opinion, so should we. One of their Sergeant Majors won the only VC of D-Day, a hardened campaigner before he ever went to France. I have often wondered if he had been on that LCA.

I lay for a moment gasping in the sand, trying to take in what, I felt, (if I should survive) would be a unique battle panorama. (Even then I had futile literary pretensions!) Mesmerised, I stared out at the vast invasion fleet making its way inexorably towards the shore. Some were still firing as they came in, at inshore targets, particularly those with tanks or self-propelled guns aboard. Airplanes were weaving in and out, in a protective cover in the skies. Some of the waxen corpses we had noticed on the way in, bobbing about like sinister corks, were now being washed ashore. The illusory nature of my security was soon shattered by a cluster of shells which fell around me. Soon I had clawed out a shallow pit in the sand with my hands. Even so, I could not resist gazing out over its rim to the shoreline. There I saw incredible sights of bravery and confusion. To my right lay the dead, grotesque figures clad in green rubber. I took these to be dead Germans; they were, in fact, our frogmen, a well-kept secret at the time. These brave men had guided the invasion fleet onto the beaches and many paid for this with their lives.

To my left, just a few feet from my hole, lay a blonde, heavily moustached tank officer with a great wound in his forehead, his dead eyes open wide. Four other tanks, which had been knocked out, lay nearby. On the edge of the sea lay wrecked and burning landing craft and sundry flaming transport. Some of the troops were trying to salvage vehicles and equipment. Wounded were being dragged up the beach or crawling away from the advancing tide. Bundles of soiled and bloodstained khaki cloth indicated the corpses, mainly of the assault troops, who had enabled us to get this far. The shell and machine-gun fire now coming down on the beach was light and ill-aimed, for as the battle moved inland the Germans were obliged to engage more pressing targets.

During the Italian invasion, I had been cut off and having seen the ordeal of the follow-up troops, badly shelled by a counter attack, I knew I must get off the beach fast. I started to run and crouch along the beach, towards the area in which my unit should be fighting. As I was dressed only in a soaked battledress, I knew I must acquire some gear quickly. With all the discarded equipment left by the dead and wounded, this was not a problem. Soon I had everything I needed. The steel helmet I picked up had been camouflaged for the desert and was soon changed for something less obvious. My progress along the beach comes back only in fragments. I vaguely remember dressing many ghastly wounds. At one stage I helped an RAMC Lt. Col. unload a waterlogged jeep, while he cursed his laggard men. The RAMC rarely go into the front line, as the infantry collect and treat their own wounded, before sending them behind the line. Near the same spot I tried to dress the blinded eyes of a screaming officer in the Dorsets. I did not try to clean any of the sand from the red pits where his eyes had been, just covered them up with a shell dressing. Just after leaving him, I stumbled on the Regimental Aid Post (RAP) of the Dorsets and went back to get him. This RAP, just off the beach, contained men of many Corps and Regiments. The MO of the Dorsets asked me to stay and help out. After a while I asked permission to leave and find my battalion, reluctantly he gave it. I knew from the briefing that the Dorsets were on our immediate left and so our men ought to be not too far away.

Around what was probably noon, I was finally creeping up a road, screened by a self-propelled gun. There were many dead Hampshires along the road so there was no doubting the direction. Many of these had been inflicted by Germans in a heavily fortified sanatorium, which had accounted for several tanks. Its main armament was, by now, silent, but some of its machine guns still active. The SP by which I was crouching opened up at the sanatorium and nearly deafened me. As I cringed, someone waved at me from the wayside ditch. I stooped to speak to him as a line of machine guns' bullets wanged on the armour, where I had been seconds before. In it was one of our stretcher-bearers with a wounded man. Dragging, crawling and crouching we carried the man back to a large captured bunker, being used as a dressing station. I was by then too exhausted and scared to go back up the road. The other man felt the same.

We met up with the remnants of the unit late in the afternoon, having recovered enough to go forward. It was three or four miles from the beach. I have not the slightest remembrance, either of the terrain or how we got there. The only thing I can recall was reporting to the MO in a small villa on the edge of Arromances. We knew him to be a brave man with an MC, which no doubt he had to live up to many times that day. He asked us angrily where we had been, probably accused us of being gutless and several other uncomplimentary things. He did calm down a bit, when he asked me about the Sgt. and the others, being casualties.

All the NCO's in the medical section had been killed or wounded during the day. He promoted from private to Sgt. an old sweat wearing two campaign medals from the N.W. India frontier, the Palestine medal and the African star. (There had been quite a lot of these regulars in the unit at one time. Magnificent soldiers but with some strange habits and almost their own language. Many had been away from England for over ten years when we came back from Italy. He had almost certainly been an NCO before and stripped for some lapse of discipline.)

By now dusk was gathering and the rest of the promotions would have to be the next day. There had been still the sound of firing as the Rifle companies took the hills of Tracy south of Arromances. This now ceased and a strange silence descended. From this final skirmish some German casualties were brought into the villa. The last one of the day being a Captain accompanied by a medical orderly. The MO examined the wound and left the Sgt and me to complete the dressing. As he left the room, the new Sgt. removed the officer's watch. That night I slept in an outhouse, supposedly guarding the orderly. It became chilly and so we pulled his blanket over us and slept. He was a canny soldier bringing his blanket with him, well pleased to be out of the war. There would be little sleep for what was left of the rifle companies on the hills. I could be with them tomorrow and had long since learned to sleep at every opportunity.

At dawn the next day the MO sent me off with a despatch rider to compile a roll of the dead and wounded. We checked not only the main RAMC clearing stations, but also many other units in the beachhead. We looked moreover in fields, houses, gardens and ditches. The list was about 200 and could not include those lost at sea or evacuated by the navy.

During this search we had a chance to see the ground covered by the battalion the previous day. It seemed a long way from Asnelles to Arromanches with broken terrain and plenty of silenced German posts. I wondered on their courage and endurance. By then we knew that the CO had been twice wounded on the beach, the second-in-command killed and the two leading companies decimated on the beach. A flail tank and some others had saved the day, clearing the mines and giving cover to the infantry. All were knocked out. This gave the follow-up companies opportunity to slip ashore covered by the tanks' hulls.

Major Warren, a surviving company commander, regrouped the battalion and devised a new plan involving fresh armour coming ashore, using their radios to get fire support from the Navy. It was certainly never that tidy, but he was awarded a well-deserved DSO. The cost had been high, perhaps not by WW1 standards, although these were almost as bad in the subsequent fighting, often with heavy casualties in a day's fighting. Our division, the 50th, were the only division to capture nearly all their objectives on D-Day. The site for the Mulberry harbour was secured, Bayeux taken on D+1 and the road towards the US army cut by our troops, denying it to the enemy. We knew nothing about Mulberry and I saw it for the first time 40 years later. It was to become the main supply port for the allied armies, particularly when the American harbour was destroyed in a storm, which did more damage to shipping than the Germans.

We got back about noon from our casualty search. The battalion was packing for a move. The depleted unit marched inland through the town of Bayeux. Those with some memory of history might have time to reflect that this lovely old town was undamaged and its glorious tapestry showed a wonderful story of an invasion going on in the other direction. Somewhere the other side of Bayeux we dug in for the night. We little knew we would stay in the line for eight weeks. A fortunate attack of malaria took me away for a couple of weeks and probably saved my life. When I got back the battalion was preparing for what was to be a dash through northern France and Belgium, as the supporting infantry to the armoured divisions. Few were left in the rifle companies of those who had landed on D-Day.

I returned for the 40th anniversary of the landing. I was interviewed for breakfast TV by a young woman, not even born in 1944. She wasn't too well briefed, half believing most of the invasion took place at Arromanches, instead of on a 5 division front. Arromanches had changed little but the countryside had lost many of its hedgerows. Certain small places like Tilly and

Hottot still produced some bad vibes. I was pleased to see a memorial to 50 Div. in the Cathedral Close at Bayeux, and two memorials to our Brigade, 231. Inf., one at Asnelles, the other at Hottot, and a street named Rue Royal Hampshire Regt. The Mayor of Asnelles invited the nine men of my regiment to lunch and gave us all a commemorative medal. These medals were far superior to the appallingly cheap medals stamped only on one side issued by our government. The march past the Queen and Prince Phillip was moving in the bright evening sunlight, which set gloriously over Arromanches.

Standing on the cliff top watching the sea stain red and purple, I asked the inevitable question of the survivor: "Why was I spared?" As I remembered the bravery of those lying in the cemeteries or those mutilated in body or mind. I knew no human being could answer that question and that one must try to do the best with one's life, after being saved by mysterious providence.

BY WATER AND FIRE

We should have charged ashore on D-Day,
Clinging to your Churchill flame-thrower.
Guns firing and flames shooting
Out of your lethal nozzle.
But the skipper, with enemy shells
Geysering the sea and exploding on the bridge,
Let your tank down into too deep water.
During that long, hard June day,
Who knows why some were spared and others lost?

Now weeks later during the
Grinding battle of the hedgerows,
With so few left in the battalion,
Who came ashore on H-Hour,
We now meet again.

They must have recovered your tank,
When the tide went out and saved you!
Now you clank up the darkening road,
That leads to the crossroads,
Where we have lost so many good men
And three brewed up tanks,
Trying to clear the SS Panzer Grenadiers
Together with two Tiger tanks,
Barricaded in the ruins of some houses.
You must have been ordered t burn them out.

As I lie in the ditch at the edge of the road,
I can just see your doomed faces

Peering from the open hatches.
I slide to the side of the tank,
Say something to try and cheer you up.
What a stupid suicide mission.

Into the gloaming the tank trundles forward
Then in an orange, fiery, flash it explodes.
We stay in the ditches all night,
Lit by the pyre of your cremation.

Perhaps they'll call up the Typhoons at dawn,
If the skies clear.
What cruel fate spared you death by water,
Only to be consumed by fire?

Tilly crossroads, Normandy 1944

DIED OF WOUNDS

They got you back to the Regimental Aid Post,
Through the heavy shellfire
That blew out the windows,
Blasted the roof tiles
And shook the old farmhouse,
Like the prey of a terrier.

All that morning they came,
Hampshires and DLI.
Ashen, ragged, bloodstained.
The walking wounded, the badly wounded.
Shattered limbs, some crudely bandaged,
Some exposed. Blood-smeared bodies and faces,
Others with air sucking out of wounds,
In chest and back.

Crawling, limping, staggering,
Desperate to get out of the line.
Some carried in by stretcher-bearers,
Others brought in by comrades,
Looking for an excuse, to get away from the front.
The wounded, some silent, some screaming, twisted, broken,
Pain mixed with relief, to be out of the line.

We got you on to the kitchen table,
Just as two salvos of Nebelwerfers
Rocked the building. We patched you up,
Then started to set your thigh
With a rifle for a splint.

I held the chloroform pad
Over your drawn and pallid face,
To blot out the pain of body and mind,
You struggled a little for breath,
Who knows what went through your anguished mind?
Then you seemed to pass into a drugged sleep.
But there was to be no awakening
From that deep, final sleep of death.

Hottot, Normandy 1944

IMPERFECT LOVE

We left the invasion beaches,
For the front line the next morning.
Then after a few days skirmishing,
Went into our first major attack.
Heavy barrage and counter barrage,
Armour grinding and milling around the hedgerows,
Burning tanks, vehicles and farmhouses,

When our time came to go forward
The whole company lay
Pinned down in a dry ditch,
Screened by a tall hedge,
Bracketed by shells and
Lashed by random machine-gun fire.

Suddenly came a rifle shot and
The cry of "Stretcher Bearer".
I crawled forward over scared riflemen,
Slit open your soiled trousers,
Saw the jagged wound in your buttock,
Spoke to your trembling friend, who
Said you asked him to inflict it.

As I plugged the hole
Another shot rang out.
I turned to see your friend
Crouching, shaking, gazing at
The blue, red hole in his palm,
Just made by him.

We lost many stretcher-bearers,
That hot, savage, summer's day.
So they sent some reluctant RAMC
Orderlies into the front line,
To get you back to the RAP.

There you were lost in the flood
Of casualties from other regiments,
Swept back in the tide of evacuation,
Your sad deeds unreported.

I saw you many months later
In a convalescent camp.
Still limping with your wound,
You avoided my gaze.

They say "Perfect love casteth out fear".
But how imperfect the love on that day
And what terror and madness,
Brought you to such an act,
Of self-violence and despair?
May God bring peace to you
Over the passing years and
All of us who cursed your anguish,
on that fearful day.

Normandy, June 1944

HE WHO WOULD VALIANT BE

You bounced into the Regimental Aid Post,
Glanced at the soiled stretchers, stacked
Against the battered, pock-marked walls,
The light coming through the blasted roof.
The graves in the front garden and
Blood caked equipment in the yard.

You gave a cheery farewell to our MO,
Now leaving, shivering and exhausted,
After weeks of combat and now malaria.
Perhaps you noticed his MC and Africa Star
And hoped to follow in his footsteps.

You tried to cheer the tired men in the RAP,
With friendly conversation and simple jokes.
You were very young, blonde and handsome,
Full of martial vigour, eager for the fray,
Keen to test your manhood and skills.

When the message came, that a fighting patrol
Was setting out at noon,
You insisted on going, despite
The Sergeant saying your place was in the RAP.

So you were there in the front line,
When the patrol left and their barrage descended,
That lethal curtain of hell.
Wailing Nebelwerfers, mortars, spandaus,
Heavies, eighty-eights and tank fire.

Shattering and shaking the earth,
Blotting out the land in smoke and fumes.

When they brought you back from the inferno,
You were mad.
Staring, unseeing eyes, flaring nostrils
And straining with terror on the stretcher,
To which they had lashed you
Like a newly captured wild beast.

Your moment of glory had been brief,
A fleeting contribution to a long war,
But you had been valiant in your way –
Perhaps saner than most of us.

Hottot, Normandy 1944

END OF RUNNING

Our company set off through
The broken hills at night,
To cut the enemy lines.
The officers stopped
In the total darkness
To compare compasses.

Most of the men fell asleep
After days without rest.
Then the company slipped away,
Leaving we two still sleeping.
We awoke just before dawn,
Went down the wahdi,
Fell over some Italians in blankets,
Took them prisoner and turned back,
Now realising the way to our lines.

Back at company HQ under shellfire,
They loaded us up with ammunition
To take to the front.
Panting and sweating we delivered
Our loads to those now cutting
The road behind the enemy lines.

But then they attacked with armoured cars,
Heavy shelling and mortaring,
Long range machine gun fire.
Lightly armed, our men retreated.
Some started to run past us in a panic
And ran down a ravine,
Shells bursting along its rims.

We went with them my friend,
Panting under the weight of weapons
Terror, thirst and fatigue,
Bursting lungs, sweat-drenched khaki drill
Under the relentless sun.
Came to a farmhouse and drank
The chilled water from the well,
The water of life, it seemed.

Now a year later you lie dead,
In the damp tunnel of a
Dark, green Normandy lane.
Sodden with the night's rain,
Washed and laid out by nature.

Few bloodstains on your broken body,
One leg missing,
Your poor corpse pitted
With fragments of a mine
You laid, but forgot in the darkness.

My friend, I gave you a poor burial –
Putting you in that can-littered trench,
But I was exhausted.
Anyway, they'll take you up eventually,
Burying you in a smart military cemetery,
Your tombstone with the Regimental crest.

But you seemed at peace,
When I covered you up
And will not need to run again in fear,
Like so many of us survivors,
Still running over the years to come.

Agira, Sicily 1943 and Hottot, Normandy 1944

MALARIAL REPRIEVE

Oh timely Malarial relapse coming,
After that terrible attack on Hottot.
Bloody, butchers' shambles in the gully,
Strewn limbs and broken men.
Streams of wounded to be tended,
My battledress soaked to the skin
With thick, cloying smell of fresh blood.
Incessant gunfire, indiscriminate death but
Successful Typhoon attacks on the Tigers,
Prisoners coming in, the battle going well.

Then that night we were all back
in the same holes as before,
German machine gun tracer reaching out,
From the corners of the fields,
Infiltrating with fiery, red fingers.

We started out to get the CO's body,
Shattered with his jeep, by an 88
Just in front of our lines,
Mercifully we were called back by the adjutant.

Now I lie on a stretcher,
In my filthy, stained battledress,
Shivering and sweating with Malaria,
A mug of water and some pills,
Is all I shall need for a few days,
Between staggering out to the latrines.

In beds, on the other side of the marquee,
Lie the badly wounded,
Waiting to be shipped home,
When they get well enough to be moved.
Down the tent at night,
A nurse in battledress passes briefly.

I don't care, I'm out of the line.
My boots are off for the first time in weeks,
I shan't have to worry about whether I shall be killed,
If I sit, or lie down, or stand up
At the wrong time.

The lice that are hatching out
In the fever heat, will have to be baked out.
Maybe they'll give me some clean underclothes.
Then when I'm better,
I'll have the first proper sleep for weeks,
Even a stroll to the local village.
Before they send me back to the line.

Hottot, Normandy 1944

A LIBERATION

After slowly clawing our way through
The Bloody Normandy hedgerows,
Suddenly it was all speed and movement, as we
Swept through the towns of Northern France.
Amiens, Arras, Lille, the killing grounds of the Great War.
Speeding past the beautifully tended acres
Of white ranked crosses, in the military cemeteries,
But now it was kisses, wine, flowers and the Marseillaise.

Then across the frontier into Belgium,
But suddenly at dawn, back into battle,
With the crack of exploding 88's.
Our anti-tank gun is knocked out,
As a German tank grinds up the village street.
Hit by a PIAT bomb.
It withdraws, shedding dead and wounded.
I go on the first patrol to check that
The village is clear, taking the pistol
And wallet from a dead German paratrooper.

Then back on the trucks, full speed to Brussells.
Flag-waving, ecstatic, singing, jubilant crowds.
Unforgettable floods of emotion, passionate release,
After long years of worry, terror and oppression.
You came into the bar where I was
Recklessly spending all my blood money.
I spoke to you hesitantly in my poor French.

You took me on a rickety tram, to buy Triple Sec.
Your husband taken to work in the Reich.

Two emotion-starved people, made love in a small wood.
For that elemental moment the war ended.
Back at the installation we should be guarding,
the Company Commander is going crazy,
Looking for the men taken into bars and houses.
"God knows what would happen if the Germans return".

I gave the Sergeant Major the rest of the money
So we could spend the night on a concrete floor.
The coarse army blankets a bed of great sensuality,
As we two young people, desperate to lose the
Shadow of war and its uncertain future,
Illuminated the darkness,
In the pleasure and oblivion of our bodies.

We exchanged addresses, as I got on the truck
The next day, to go to Antwerp and the front,
But we never met again.

Brussells, 1944

WHO WANTS TO DIE ON VE DAY?

Who wants to die in the last days
Of a long hard war?
It was never a conflict of blind patriotism,
Only something to be endured with stoicism,
To survive, if possible with some dignity.

In the cold, wet Belgian barracks,
Now an Infantry Reinforcement Depot,
Scarred veterans, young unbloodied recruits,
Re-mustered RAF, AA and Navy personnel,
Hastily retrained as reluctant infantrymen,
Eagerly devour any rumour which
Promises a speedy end to the fighting.

In the ex-cavalry, horse training ring,
Scores fall in for the sick parades,
Hoping to delay posting to the front,
Only to be tongue lashed with bitter humour.
Their imagined ailments ordered to be
Shouted out loud for all to hear.
In the mess halls, deserters hide in the queues,
Gulping furtive meals and dodging the MP's.

Men slip into the camp cinema for hours,
Skulk around the town in the rain,
Or shelter gloomily under the trees,
Of the 1914 German war cemetery,
With its Iron Cross headstones,
To avoid parades and fatigues.

Each night, like fitful fireflies,
The matches flicker in the darkness,
Lighting up the lists of men
Posted to any of the Regiments up the line,
Depleted by the fighting.
So much for the Regimental system.

But still in my memory, images linger
Of the burning tanks and our dead riflemen,
Lying on the dark, pine forest floor,
Across the Rhine, in the last days
Before ceasefire.

Belgium and Germany, 1945

ALFIE BOLLEN

I am going to write about a young man I knew briefly, for about seven years between 1937 and 1944. Historians vary in their interpretations of history, favouring politics, economics, science, religion and many other factors, but history is also individual stories, imposed on the fabric of time.

I digress from this biography, so we return to the young man, Alfie, whose short history and mine coincided. We met when my family – mother and two sisters, moved from unfurnished rooms in Kentish Town in London, to a purpose-built flat between Mornington Crescent and Albany Street. My father had died when I was seven in 1930. These were the years of the great Depression, affecting us, and many other people, with grinding poverty. The flats were owned by the Crown and were acquired by the influence of a wealthy woman my mother 'did for'. To us, the flat was the height of luxury with a boarded-over bath in the kitchen, electric stove and electric iron. The family finances improved as we were all working, although my brother remained in the army, where he had enlisted aged fourteen. Army recruitment was strong due to the unemployment in the 1930's.

We attended the local church opposite Great Portland Street underground station, now an Anglican bookstore. As well as the services, there was the customary social side. The curate at the time was Edward Carpenter, later to become Dean of Westminster Abbey and radical in his theology. This was the time when Archbishop Temple was a paid up member of the old Labour party. Edward prepared us for confirmation in St. Paul's Cathedral. Alfie didn't stay the course. I also joined the badminton club and transferred to the scout troop, although I was beginning to feel a little old for scouting. Alfie was a member of the badminton club and scouts and we were both in awe of Gladys, the belle of the club, then way out of our league. Alfie liked to come to our flat, to get warm and have the occasional meal and also for the company – he was a sociable lad. I also got involved with the Young Communist league. The Depression, the indifference of the government of fascism and my friends in the sixth form, were all instrumental in my membership. In 1941 I raised the red flag over one of the lions in Trafalgar Square in a demo urging the government to open the second front. I little knew I would end up taking part in three invasions. Three other of my friends from the YCL did not survive the war.

To come back to Alfie: we were both 17 and he was living just off Camden High Street in lodgings with his father, a window cleaner, whose puffy red face revealed his fondness for beer. It is worth remembering that few people at that time owned any property, most rented. There was also another brother from Alfie's father's broken marriage (rare at the time). Alfie certainly left school at 14, the leaving age of most. Thanks to my mother, I left school at 16 with the school certificate obtained at an LCC central technical school. (These schools, set up despite government hostility, were probably the most suitable for a modern society. They were all closed in 1948.) Alfie was fairly well spoken, blond haired and blue eyed and very presentable. He acquired a long blue coat and black homburg hat later in the blitz.

His younger brother was killed in an air raid while in an amusement arcade in Tottenham Court Road. I went to the funeral and wake which was fairly elaborate for the times. I was always amazed at the way most people coped with bereavement in wartime. I lost my mother and younger sister in the blitz and my brother later in Burma. Perhaps they coped because people were so pleased to still be alive themselves and of course shared the horrors.

In 1940, Alfie and I joined the ARP as scout messengers to get our ARP badges. The post was in Fitzroy Square and was commanded by a World War 1 veteran. Being so near Soho, it was manned by a rare collection of would-be actors, writers and painters. First Aid was taught by a large, dramatic nurse who had served in the Spanish civil war; all in all, not a bad experience for young lads. Nothing happened for a year of the war. France and Britain threw away the chance to attack German which was fighting Poland. However, because of the way the allies had been trained and led, perhaps the result would have been the same. At all events, Alfie and I learned to play a good game of table tennis and billiards in the phoney war period.

Then the war started in earnest: Dunkirk, the Battle of Britain and the almost nightly bombing of London, which lasted for nearly six months. The night sky over the city burned a fiery red, visible for miles and blazing gas mains flared in the streets. The buses were tossed aside like toys or lay in great bomb holes. Then parachute mines were often seen suspended from church steeples. Most Londoners had the choice of an Anderson shelter in the backyard or one of the few public shelters. Some simply sheltered under the stairs in their homes or went in large numbers to the Underground. The Anti aircraft artillery sited in the parks and open spaces fired most of the hours of darkness and fragments of shells fell like hail. Eventually, the better shelters developed entertainment, toilets and canteens. Alfie and I made the rounds of the best of the dances and singsongs – collective singing was a big feature of wartime culture. We seemed quite unafraid of the danger at the time despite having to help with some gruesome casualties. We also got by on very little sleep, which was of course preparation for worse horrors of front line soldiering, later on in the war. Of course there was virtually no counselling for trauma at the time.

Back to 1940/41s. Alfie's and my undoing came when we were posted as shelter marshals at a large surface shelter behind Warren Street underground station. There were a few exciting moments fighting fires in the car showrooms, but it was mostly boring and freezing cold. We were also too young to control the revellers and tended to join them. Finally we took up with two attractive girls and although our snogging was high on frustration and low on satisfaction, it incurred the wrath of the post commander. We were sacked and handed in our equipment at ARP HQ in Malet Street, a location which was to become familiar after 1946 when I was a Librarian, and student at University College.

Alfie and I lost touch after my home was bombed out by a parachute mine. My older sister and I, who survived, went to live in two gas lit rooms in Tufnell Park. In the year before I went into the army, we went to the Paramount dance hall in Tottenham Court Road most evenings. I suppose it was our bereavement therapy. Being in a semi basement, it gave an illusion of safety. It was furnished like one of the Hollywood dream factory nightclubs. It also probably had the best swing bands available in the UK. When the Yanks came to the UK the fantasy was complete. The bands of Miller, James and Goodman still evoke the bittersweet memories of this period. It was here I met Gladys of the badminton club again, and by then I had become a reasonable dancer and something of a dancehall flaneur. My introduction to sex took place in her parents' flat, while they were in the shelter. I was then working in a public library in Camden, vainly trying to study for the Library Association exams.

Having been so-called trained by the army, I went around the Cape to Egypt, two months of unforgettable squalor, then took part in the Sicily and Italy invasions. I was lucky being posted to an experienced infantry battalion. We were pulled out of the line in Italy and told that the whole division with two others was going home for the invasion of Europe. I was fortunate because I rated my chances as low in getting through two winter campaigns in Italy. The invasion was the "better" option. In the UK, we had leave and I went back home. I went to the Paramount and also saw Gladys, married with a baby, so therefore was now off limits. During that leave I was just getting off a bus in Camden Town when I almost put my hand on Alfie's shoulder. He was in uniform, I believe it was the Buffs, and he looked very smart. We met that evening for a drink – there was a lot to tell each other.

Alfie said the army had changed his life: he was fit, had gained confidence and loved the comradeship. It was not an unfamiliar story for working class lads. He was going to become a regular and had volunteered for the paras. We both went to the Paramount and had a few beers, not many as the infantry were the worst paid of the services. I was wounded in September 1944 and came back to the UK. Soon after, the Arnhem operation took place during which Alfie was killed. I can't imagine the confusion and terror for a young soldier in this, his first battle. My sister, staying later with a German friend in Holland, sent me a photograph of his grave. She wrote: 'It is very near the border, we were surprised.'

I have thought deeply about the Arnhem operation since. It even had Brigadier Urquhart in command under whom we had served in Sicily and Italy. In September 1944, our division, the 50th infantry, accompanied the 11th armoured and 6th Guards on the offensive towards Arras and Lille, past many of the great cemeteries of WW1, then on to Brussels and Antwerp. The joy of liberation on the faces of the people was unforgettable and made all the fighting seem worthwhile. After the war, the leading German generals said they expected a big push in the direction of Arnhem, but of a much larger force. The allies had about 60 divisions in France and Belgium, but our Generals claimed that supplies were a problem. Surely Bomber Command could have been persuaded to take this on? Our army in Burma, with RAF support, managed to supply their troops over hundreds of miles of jungle, mud tracks and rivers bigger than the Rhine. Just over a month after Arnhem, the Americans lost about 100,000 men, making a frontal assault on the Hurtgen forest and Aachen. That force, with its tanks and equipment, would have ensured the success of the Arnhem operation. This strategic incompetence and foolish rivalry among the allied generals cost thousands of lives in the extended war and of course in the occupied countries, by hunger, bombing and in the death camps. Arnhem was not just a failure of an operation but a serious failure of generalship. Eisenhower, the overall commander, was later to become president of the USA.

When I was on leave later from Germany, I went to see Alfie's mother. It was big mistake because it only drew attention to my good fortune in surviving and Alfie's sad fate. Whatever the circumstances of his death, to me he had been a hero and I hope his mother drew comfort from this.

A CRACK AT THE HUN

The war in Europe was drawing to a close. It was evident it should be over in a few weeks. The draft from the UK arrived at Bourg Leopold in northern Belgium, under the command of a young subaltern aged about nineteen. It had taken them nearly three days to get from Calais in cattle trucks. They did not complain, it was three days less at the front. It was only the young Officer who was keen "to have a crack at the Hun". This he had repeated endlessly during the drill parades and route marches, which formed their useless training.

The draft was 50% veterans returning after wounds and 50% rookie eighteen year olds. Nothing had been imparted to the eighteen year olds which would help them. Digging in, use of weapons, operating with tanks, not even the primitive battle drill, picked up mainly from the Germans. The enemy, which used their superior infantry weapons in attack and defence, were rarely matched and the army would end the war, in the way it had been conducted most of the time, by weight of numbers and material.

While marching up the snow-bound coast before coming to France, they had heard the sound of the new RAF jet fighters in testing. They would not have been able to articulate the differences between the services, but were proud of the long record of success of the airmen. They little knew, or perhaps cared less that the RAF training tactics, equipment and technology had kept pace with the Germans throughout the war. The officer corps of the RAF had trained to fight a modern war. The army was trained for 1914/18 and hardly any senior officer in the army had any experience of armoured warfare, not even those who would become successful generals. Almost like having senior RAF officers without flying experience. All the veterans could say to the rookies about combat was, "*Ignore this rubbish training and pick it up from the old hands at the front*".

As soon as the men arrived and secured their beds, they went to the mess hall. Geoff, a dark, wiry man, wearing the Africa Star ribbon, stroked his stubble. Suddenly he saw someone in the queue he knew. It was John Dale, a tall, thin man with a long clown's face, full of comic expression, with a gingery, drooping moustache. John had fought at Alamein and been posted to Geoff's regiment, when his was disbanded. Two years ago they had been company runners together. They both said simultaneously, "Do you remember?" Laughingly, they recalled a terrifying night run they had made through a heavy German barrage to get help, amazed to be still alive.

Geoff said "I just missed you at Seagate. What a dump! Fancy sending those kids over here after that." "Same when I was there, miserable shower. Wouldn't let some blokes have sleeping out passes when they brought their wives down. Wonderful way of rewarding your fighting men, the bastards, bet they had theirs on tap. As for the kids it was the same with us, we were just lucky being sent to a good mob. They should clear out these training units and send them up the line." replied John.

Geoff asked, "What's the low down on this place? I saw Kelly and Carter in the grub queue, didn't want to talk to me, they looked very miserable." "Well mate, they're both on the trot, MP's will catch up with them soon, they're always around." Geoff looked anxious. "Bates and Miller were on my draft, let out of gaol, to go back up the line. Can't see them sticking it out. What's with the old mob, whole division broken up I hear?" "That's right, Geoff, been sent back to blighty to be reformed." "Shame after the fighting record it had, Desert, Italy, Normandy landing. Not hat hardly any made it to all these places. But I shall miss the old mob." John pulled his moustache. "Don't care where I go, my division was broken up after Alamein, when I came to your lot." Geoff inched up the queue. "When we got wounded on the Albert Canal, I thought the war would be over then. There must have been a cock-up with the Brass. Hardly saw a Jerry after we left Normandy." "Yes mate, and there's been quite a few cock-ups since. Yanks are no better than us with all their men and gear."

Geoff pointed to a group of soldiers noisily chatting on the end table of the mess hall, as they sat down with their stew. "They seem to be in high spirits." "The reluctant infantry, mate, ex-navy, RAF ground staff and Ack Ack, don't need them at this stage of the war." Geoff looked across at them. "They're not youngsters, must have been in the services for years, it'll be a shock for them when they get up the line." "Right, mate, though there's quite a few fly buggers amongst them, trying to dodge the column." "Not so desperate as those two pathetic sods, who shot each other, when we crouched in that ditch under fire near Hottot." said Geoff.

It was dark as they made their way back to the hut. In front of each company office stood a knot of soldiers striking matches. John pointed at them "Checking their postings to the front. There's another battalion of our mob at the front, but they're overstrength with guys making their way back to the front from our lot." "You surprise me after what you've said, that anyone is volunteering to get back up the line". "Kidding themselves, mate, that they'd be safe with a mob wearing the same cap badge, Jerries don't seem to have any special regiments except their paras, they don't do so bad." "What do you do here, while you wait for posting?" "Get out of camp fast mate, to avoid fatigues and if it's raining, go to the camp cinema. Couldn't say how many times I've seen some films. There's a big Jerry cemetery from the Great War, quite near if you want cheering up. If you want a big laugh on the other hand, go sick, it's one of the camp sights."

The next day Geoff reported sick. He was surprised there was so little formality. He went to the main parade ground and joined about 250 men. Eventually a Sergeant, with two others in attendance, took the parade. The marching was orderly, just about, but hardly soldierly. They halted outside a large, round building. It wasn't an M.I. room. Inside was a large, sanded ring. The smell of horses pervaded and the only light came from windows set high in the walls. It was the horse-breaking ring of a Belgian Cavalry barracks. The parade shuffled inside and stood around.

The Sergeant taking the parade formed them into a large circle and two chairs were placed in the centre. Presently a buzz of excitement went through the ranks, as an MO and RAMC corporal came in. The corporal wrestled with the unwieldy list of all the men on the parade. The Sergeant called the men to attention and a pathetic muffled motion stirred the sand. "At ease. When you name is called, I want you to sit in this chair," (he pointed) "I'll be in the other. I want you to tell me what's the matter, clearly, so everyone can hear plainly. Shout if necessary," said the MO.

The first man out sat down. "Let's see, I gave you three days excused duty, are you better now?" "Not really Sir, I still get the runs." "Too bad, Laddie," said the MO in his Scot's dialect. "You can run off up the front. Medicine and Duty and see you take the pills this time." A titter ran around the circle. The next patient came and sat down self-consciously. The whispered symptoms could not be heard. "Speak up Laddie, we can't all hear." "It's my piles, Sir." said the victim in a louder voice. "Piles, nothing to be ashamed of, Royalty have them, I'll give you some ointment. Medicine and duty." Next was a large, fresh-faced soldier, obviously bursting with health. "Terrible wind, Sir, gives me awful pains in the night." "Show me where," said the MO. The patient pointed vaguely in the abdominal region. "If we put every soldier to bed that farted a bit, there'd be no army. Medicine and duty."

An old soldier, wearing the campaign ribbons of India and Palestine came next. His face was full of guile and he had taken the trouble to limp up to the chair. "It's me back, hurts me to carry equipment." "How did you get on the boat and train to come here Laddie?" "Oh, it's only come on since I arrived here Sir." "Sergeant, did you see this man on parade?" "Yes Sir, I noticed him because of his ribbons." "Don't play the old soldier with me, Laddie." The Sergeant would have told me if he'd see you limping on parade. We weren't born yesterday. Medicine and Duty." It was highly improbable that the MO had seen the Sgt before, as they were changed virtually daily.

The reluctant infantry, drafted in from the other services, had made a good showing among the veterans and in some cases had better rehearsed stories. Geoff wished he could have recorded some of the performances, which strained all human ingenuity. Coughs, colds, stomachache, backaches, feet trouble, dizzy spells, fainting fits, pains around the heart and lungs. Most were quickly pronounced fit. One with a very high temperature was allowed "to bed down". A flushed solider wearing the ribbon of the Africa star, claiming to have a relapse of malaria, then had his temperature taken. "Just over normal Laddie, breathe on me, haven't been chewing cordite have you? Medicine and Duty. If it gets worse, report to your MO when you get to your battalion."

Sprinkled among the runners were three VD cases. The first two were greeted with roars of laughter and shouts of "lucky sod". The third, a Geordie, gained the biggest applause. He had to repeat his story twice and display his member. "Was bitten by a dog, when I was taking a slash, Sir." Even the MO was taken aback. He muttered "Rabies may be, but VD never. Stand with the other three." Geoff was to meet the soldier in Germany after the war. The name 'Slash Connor' was still sticking to him.

In between came the 'bomb happy cases'. Soldiers suffering what was once called shell shock, in the US army combat fatigue. The British army would only grudgingly accept this, if the soldier had broken down at the front and then usually only if the person had a long record of combat. One of the men on parade, who came with a mixture of fear, inspired acting and desperation, conjured up such a series of nightmares, based on his battle experiences, real or imagined, that he was given 3 days excused duty, to general approval. The man in front of Geoff had been wounded five times. He was small, shrunken in body and mind, and ex Durham miner, who had been through all the campaigns of his division, an obvious case for treatment. The MO said, "No army rule to say you can't be wounded 50 times and anyway you have to report sick with this at the front". Nevertheless, he gave the man ten days excused duties, which raised a small cheer.

Geoff felt slightly ashamed when it came to his turn and stuttered something about his old leg wound hurting him. "Show me Laddie, perfectly healed and sound, don't waste my time soldier." The last man in the parade was wearing gym shoes. "What are you doing wearing gym shoes Laddie? Shouldn't even have them on the scale of equipment you're supposed to be on." The soldier already had his sock and shoe off and revealing a barely-healed scar, he said nothing. "Go and join the others." He indicated the VD and other genuine patients.

They all fell in outside, laughing and joking and they were marched back to the main parade ground to be dismissed. They had attempted to buck the system, had been entertained and no matter if the Hippocratic oath had been bent, or frequently broken, were now reasonably accepting of their future fate.

Back in the hut, Geoff said down on John's bed. "What a pathetic circus and all this taking place on the winning side." "Well, mate, nobody wants to get killed in the last few days. I expect that applies to the Jerries as well as us, judging by the rate they are surrendering. We don't have that option." Geoff grinned. "What did you cook up when it was your turn? Don't tell me you didn't try?" "You remember I got that piece of a bullet in my forehead? Told the MO it was giving me a headache. He said, Laddie, you must have been nursing that for a long time, don't give me that one. Medicine and Duty and aspirin." Geoff looked thoughtful. "He's got an impossible job really, I can only say it was a brilliant piece of applied psychology." "I don't know quite what that means, mate. I don't think he would be too sure as well, but he's a very canny Scot."

BASE WALLAHS

The two sergeants sat on opposite beds in a small German barrack room. It was November 1945. There were two large wardrobes and a small table. It was very warm although snow could be seen falling through the window. Ian, a tall, slim man, about 35 with dark eyes and a long face, spoke first.

"Can't get over seeing you in the VD clinic. Well, what's the verdict?"

"It was only a test, it's OK Ian, thank God. Picked up a dose of guntack from some quite respectable woman in Munster. Found out later she had come from Berlin, been raped by the Russkies. I've only been here a fortnight." The speaker, Tony a thickset smaller man with a reddish complexion, settled back on the bed. Ian continued "I've been here for four months, Tony. It was a corps HQ, then expanded to administer to a part of Germany the size of Ireland. There are loads of Sergeants and Officers, not to mention military government officials and stacks of batmen for the officers. No wonder we didn't see each other". Tony yawned.

"They have a bit of a problem now, being worried about the Russians. They won't speed up demob and have a surplus of NCO's. It's the same in the RAF, they never made up their minds who should be air crew officers or NCO's."

Ian coughed, "I only went with one fraulein but got so scared afterwards, with all the VD around, I got to looking at my prick by torchlight. Don't touch the frat now."

"Serves you right, always on about your wonderful wife. My missus asked for a divorce, not like your marriage. Only got married to stop her nagging, just before D-Day. The first letter I got after we landed, she wrote about how she'd found this wonderful RAF bloke and fallen in love...bloody ground staff, never left the UK.

Did me a favour really."

"Well, Tony, there are so many of you discarded blokes, it's become a legal routine for the army. You'll soon be free. My wife was good to me when I got back to the UK after being wounded at Hottot; helped pull me through."

"Yes, you looked terrible, I didn't know if you'd ever come back. Quite surprised to see you here. Sorry I didn't write; I was never much of a writer. You're the brainy one, always writing to the papers and MPs. Wonder you didn't get into trouble. Anyway, sorry about not writing, Ian."

"I got depressed as well, Tony. Relieved to get away from the front, but a bit guilty."

"That was a bad day when you got hit Ian. We lost about a hundred and fifty men, but we took Hotttot and then they pulled us out. I believe it was a bit of a shambles after the CO was killed."

"They shipped me out from Arromanches. It was a bit different from D-Day. They have a big artificial harbour there now, swarming with base wallahs."

"I had a relapse of malaria soon after Hottot, Ian. Kept me out of the line for a bit, hardly any of the old hands left in the rifle companies when I got back. Got promoted Sergeant, when they were hard up for experienced NCO's. We saw a lot of those Great War cemeteries when we got out of Normandy. Not a cheering sight when you don't know what might be around the next bend. Best bit of the war really, was to see the relief on the civvies' faces, after the occupation."

Ian smiled, "I saw some of it on the newsreels. It seemed all wine, women and song from that. Not much fighting then?" "We had a bit of a scrap just outside Brussells. We lost one man. They had about six. Blasted their tank with our PIAT, didn't stop the tank retreating with the rest of them. One of the Jerries was dying – only kept together by the rags of his uniform. I picked up a pistol and quite a bit of French money from one of them. Easy come, easy go – spent most of it in Brussells."

"How long did you stay in there, Tony?"

"Just a night. The town went crazy with joy, half the company went missing, blokes being dragged into houses for drinks, food or the other, for all I know."

"I suppose that included you! Good job Jerry didn't counterattack."

"After we left Antwerp, I got a light head wound – felt terrible with the blood pouring down over my face, I thought I'd had it. It was a piece of a bullet. It's still there, despite being flown back to blighty on a Dakota."

"Typical of the army to fly you back and then leave it in. I shouldn't say that, Tony, because I had marvellous treatment, but I didn't feel right when they shipped me out again."

"Yeah, they were getting desperate for infantry then. All those ex-Navy AA and RAF drafted into the PBI all going sick. It was obvious the war would end soon, but nobody wants to get killed just before the end."

"That's true, but they did pick up my condition and downgraded me, putting me in the RASC and sending me to 1st Corps HQ. They talk a lot of rubbish about regiments. When they want reinforcements badly, you go anywhere to replace the casualties."

"I see you're in the RASC like me now. We were both corporals at Hottot. They gave me the extra tape here. I heard about the break-up of 50 div when I was in the reinforcement camp. Not that many of the desert veterans were left. What happened to you?"

"Well, Ian, I went up the line with this Welsh mob – not that there were many Welshman in it. It was the time of the Rhine crossing. I felt quite good the first couple of days. Not too bad, most jerries packing it in, except for a few fanatics. They hadn't got much artillery except 88's. I volunteered to go through a company of the Rifle Brigade to help the crew of a tank, knocked out and burning at the end of a wooded track. It was bad seeing those dead blokes of the RB lying in the wood, so near to the end of the war. The driver of the troop carrier got the wind up, jumped out and scarpered. Then the carrier got blasted."

"So you got wounded again?"

"Not really, just shaken. I went back to the MO of the armoured unit. He asked me a few questions about my previous campaigns. He said "I think you've had enough for the time being, Sergeant.' Sent me back to a hospital for bomb happy cases. If the old Battalion had been still around I suspect I would have made my way back. As it was, I allowed myself to be downgraded and eventually accepted it."

"Don't take it to heart, Tony. Reckon I was finished, I just had a better excuse than you."

"Couldn't believe it when I got here. Good food in the mess, better in the Sergeants' restaurant in town. All this is free, best booze in the mess bar, scotch, gin, brandy, strong lager, no wonder some of these guys are hitting it. Then we get this amazing booze allowance, champagne, spirits, wine, cheap fags. All you need is to sell part of it and you're loaded. You can even buy goods in the NAAFI to send home. It's another world to the infantry."

"What's more, Tony, some of the blokes here boast they have never worn boots since basic training. The defence company are the only real soldiers here. And all this booze is the real stuff – Cliquot, Vat 69, you would never afford this champagne at home. God knows how some of them will settle down when they get demobbed."

Tony grinned. "You can't tell me the army brass don't know it's going on, with hardly anybody drawing pay and still taking German money home to change at the leave camps. We all know that the QMs fiddled, even in wartime. We rarely got a rum ration, even in wet weather and things were worse, the further you got behind the lines. You hear stories about the RAF shipping heavy stuff back home. It's all much more corrupt now."

Ian looked out at the snow.

"The odds against us sitting here a year ago must have seemed slim. So many good chaps gone west, we just survived each day. Never though we'd be RACS Sergeants. Our old platoon Sergeant always called them the ASC - never regarded them as real soldiers.

He was different to the Sergeants in basic training, patient, very brave: MM, and supportive to us raw soldiers. Just the kind you need to train young recruits when they get called up. He was killed a fortnight after we landed. Can you believe it, Ian, I met a bloke who got promoted on our basic training platoon to Lance Corporal and he made a pass at me leaving the mess one night. I realised then the reason he stayed in Blighty all the war was because that old India wallah Sergeant was screwing him. I just shoved him down into the snow, the pathetic sod. It's the officers' fault really, leaving all the training to the NCO's in these places, not like our old mob. You could have been an officer, Ian. Good education, dedicated to wiping out fascism and all that stuff."

"Not been to the right public school Tony. Anyway, I don't know how I'd have felt, knowing the men were sweating out on the troop-decks like pigs, going around the Cape, while the officers were in cabins having chef-style grub. But at least they were usually brave."

"I'm not sure they were always brave, but sometimes foolhardy. I often felt better with a good platoon Sergeant. Do you remember that officer in Normandy, in charge of the signals platoon? Got someone to dig a hole under the armoured signal truck, one of the company signallers told me, and wouldn't come out. They sent him home."

Ian offered Tony a cigarette but he refused it. "When I heard about the Jerry defeat in Normandy and the capture of Paris and Brussels, when I was lying in hospital, I thought the war would soon be over. What a mess the brass must have made of things with such a superiority of men, guns, tanks and aircraft."

"Yeah. A lot of good men and civilians died because of that, Ian. Perhaps one day someone will write up the truth about it, together with the Arnhem cock-up."

"I was worried when I first saw you here, Tony, but most of the Sergeants are quite good blokes. They will respect you for having been in the fighting, particularly with your MM."

"You needn't worry Ian, I'm not proud anymore. It's all luck or fate, we might have been in their shoes, but I wouldn't have missed our part of the war for anything."

"Never be another war like ours Tony. With this atom bomb, the Army will be small, highly trained and properly equipped. It's a new era. We've talked a lot about the changes we want when we get back home. End of all that poverty, poor health provision, unemployment, class prejudice and lousy education for working people."

"I expect you'll get some changes. Everybody's a bit Bolshie right now and they haven't seen the Tory press for many years. You taught me that. Those at the top will take much more shifting than you think. As for the PBI, they'll still be needed to go in and clear up the mess in the end. With all that bombing and shelling, Jerry was still there shooting back from the ruins."

ARROMANCHES RE-VISITED

The Sun sets yellow-mauve, over the sky and sea,
Touching the hills beyond Arromanches and Tracy.
I stand in the square, a soft wind in my face,
Black stumps of Mulberry still mark the place
Where thousands once came over to fight,
For a cause they believed was just and right.
Today the parade of veterans, still proud and erect
Marched past the Queen, the Prince and others elect.

Now all is stillness, silent the music and cheers,
Time for memories or reflections, after long years.
So forty years later and by many a strange chance,
I walk the streets of this small port in France.
You were our objective of that hard, longest day
And to capture the town a high price we would pay.

They fell in the sea, the sand, field and lane,
Some dying swiftly, but others in fearful pain.
There was no pity in the air, sea or land at that time
Nor later in the hedgerows, on that bloody battle line.
But for you my dear friend, claimed by the sea
And not marked by a grave, in any war cemetery,
I lit a candle in Bayeux Cathedral for you today
And together with a French family, kneeled to pray.

Arromanches, 40th Anniversary of D-Day,
6th June 1984

'Peace I leave with you, my peace I give unto you: not as the world giveth, give I unto you. Let not your heart be troubled, neither let it be afraid'

Holy Bible (K.J.V.) John 14:27

FAMILY

Above: Father, mother, brother Eric, sisters Ivy, Eve and Denny. Malta 1923

Left: Ivy and Den, first leave after end of World War II

FATHER

Frank William Hawes born 1891
Son of London cabinet maker.
Educated by the London School Board.
Worked as a Junior Clerk in a solicitors office,
Copied law documents with a beautiful copper plate hand.

Great talker, keen Edwardian club cyclist.
Suffered from a weak heart after a bout of rheumatic fever.
Seduced Daisy Louise Wright, born 1892,
Daughter of a London Engine Driver,
Who had been educated at a Grammar School, for prospective teacher.
Hastily married with much bad feeling on the part of bride's family.

Couple subsequently had three other children,
Were extremely in love all their married life,
Except when he would stay in the Sergeants' mess
Chatting and drinking lemonade, being a teetotaller.

Frank enlisted in the army during WW1, but weak heart made him remain in UK.
Was placed in the Pay Corps, stationed in London.
Remained in the army after the armistice, with rank of Sergeant.
Tall, fair, smart in uniform, polished brass buttons and badges,
Shining boots, pressed khaki, glittering Sergeant's stripes.
Loved the camaraderie of service life and the mess,
But did not experience the rawness of Regimental life,
Or the horror of the front line.
Both sons would discover this in the next conflict.

Upset some of his seniors, by his sense of justice and commonsense.
Not always as popular as he would have liked.
Was posted to Shanghai, then to Malta, where his family joined him.
Loved swimming and playing in the sea, with the children.

In Devon where later stationed, fond of taking kids on long walks.
Trips on trains and charabancs, to local sights.
Was very successful with an allotment, to supplement meagre pay.
Insisted on seeing the children smartly turned out,
All shoes were polished by the younger children.
Loved to hole up in the bedroom with the wife,
With sweets and 'News of the World', Sunday afternoons,
While the kids went off to Salvation Army Temple.

Great sense of fun guaranteed to make any social occasion a success.
Birthday parties and Christmas made magic by his presence.
Had serious side as a thoughtful Edwardian liberal,
While Daisy a mild conservative, mistrustful of Stalin,
Even during the praise for the USSR in WW2.
Frank took great interest in the children's schooling,
Remembering his own struggles to improve his education,
Through the army, to gain promotion.

Died suddenly aged 40 in the middle of the night.
Had spent the previous evening with the youngest son Dennis,
Drawing life-like horses to amuse and instruct him.
Frank my wonderful, warm father,
I missed you then and have done all my life.

Folkestone, May 1986

MOTHER

Daisy Louise Hawes nee Wright,
Born 1892, engine driver father.
Educated at local Grammar school.
Married Frank, Pay Corps private during WW1.
He stayed on to become regular Sergeant after the war,
and died suddenly with heart attack in 1930,
Daisy moved to London to be near their families.
Alas, sometimes, had to give them assistance.

Eldest boy went for a soldier, girl domestic service.
No savings, survived on Widow's pension, no service pension,
Frank's death being strictly civilian.
No household effects, army had supplied them.
Bought some second-hand beds, table, chairs,
Orange crates for other storage.
Lived at first in leaky, urine-smelling tenements.
Was a great homemaker, despite unpromising circumstances.

Worked as daily char, shop assistant, domestic servant.
Still good-looking, had some male friends,
Discreetly handled for sake of the family.
Eldest daughter, Ivy, eventually came home.
Youngest daughter, Eve, found good job as a secretary.
Eldest brother Eric stayed in the Royal Engineers.
Youngest boy Dennis scraped into a London Central School.

Improvement in income made it possible to rent,
With some influence from Daisy's employer, a better apartment.
Acquired electric light, cooker and iron.

Bath in the kitchen covered with boards.
Step up from the tin bath, in front of the fire.
Diet now became more varied and sustaining.

Daisy kept up Frank's tradition of family discussion,
Not only on domestic issues, but the world as she saw it.
Needed to enlist help of Headmaster at the Central School,
Dennis was getting out of hand without Frank,
But, with best intention, over-protected Dennis,
Three women with a young boy not an ideal situation.
Discouraged rougher sports. Dennis had no bicycle,
Even in the more affluent days.

Daisy had great charm, intelligence and a sympathetic ear.
The apartment was often full of relations and neighbours,
Down on their luck financially and emotionally.
Taught her children about sex, sensibly and realistically.
Didn't stop the younger one getting into trouble,
Daisy's charm with local doctor, resolved it.

Adored her son in the army, Eric,
Which was not surprising, given his array of talents.
His leaves were always a great time for rejoicing,
Recounting his adventures, fierce political debate
Special treats, long walks around London,
Visits to bookshops, museums, parks, swimming pools.
Eric loved music, art and social justice, lamb chops
And dressing up in an eiderdown as the Archbishop of Malta.
How would Daisy have coped with his death later in Burma?

One clear March night in 1941, a solitary German plane glided over
The block, planting a mine which floated down, silently to explode
Devastatingly and lethally.
Dennis on ARP watch helped Ivy from the rubble,
Both miraculously safe in body, scarred in mind.

Daisy and Eve, dead and entombed.
Their spirit has stayed with us ever since.
Daisy, great protective mother, gentle but firm,
Caring and understanding person, reader and debater,
Perceptive woman greatly in advance of her time.
What amazing grace, that you were our mother.

TO IVY

Ivy, what you mean to me
Is something I can never be.
Your quiet courage, gentle face
Great loyalty in time and place,
A life of difficulty and strife
But always full of joy and life.
Balance of body, mind and heart,
With time for nature, man and art,
Always ready to have a go
At something new you hardly know.
Not like some that I could mention –
Full of half-baked good intention.
Richness of spirit, lively thought
And with feelings finely wrought.
Those few hours in town we share
Are precious for their mutual care,
And so valued for me is the time we meet
It goes in a way that's strangely fleet.
So please forgive me for the pain
I've often brought you, more than gain.
Many things that I cannot repay
Although I live to Judgement day.
And it's very plain to me
That often with God's eyes you see.
Who works through you in many ways,
Helping you through the hard, dark days.
So please pray for me, dear sister of mine
That through my soul Christ's light will shine.

Folkestone, September 1991

NATURE

Folkestone from the Dover cliffs

The Warren and Folkestone cliffs towards Dover

WIND FROM THE STRAIGHTS

East wind, beast wind, savage wild wind,
Numbing the body, the heart and the mind,
Scouring the valleys, the hills and the roads,
Piercing the soul, with sharp, stabbing goads.
Watering the eye and freezing the feet.
Taunting us all, with the snow and sleet.
Blocking the pipe, the road and rail,
Landscape smothered with whitened mail.
Chilling the young, destroying the old,
Human fragility mocked by the cold.
How slender our life lines, are sadly revealed,
Drifts piling on pathways, like arteries congealed.
So sparkling your face on the field and the hedge,
But bleak lies the land, 'neath your bitter edge.

Folkestone, January, 1987

HOLY INNOCENTS

Gaunt, spindly trees, circular fretted shapes on the hillside.
Colours of brown-blue, flecked with splashes of evergreenery.
Valleys strangely as yet unscarred by winter's bitter tide.
Ribbons of grey roads, cutting the Kentish downs to Canterbury.
The Cathedral, beauty of stone, voice, vessel and stained glass,
Mysterious, simple, intricate forms, reflecting heaven's harmonies.
Where irridescent shafts of light, from subtle colours are cast.
Why do we deny ourselves God's wish to share in all these glories?
Filling our lives with futile work, which we dare not cease,
Toiling often for some selfish gain, or in some foolish cause.
But this day of Holy Innocents, has brought me to some peace
Moments of stillness and illumination, before eternity to pause
And Stella with her sons, gentle and calm on Christmas night,
A tender and tranquil time, which puts my fears to flight.

Folkestone, December 1987

MID WINTER SUNSHINE

Frost at night, then bright sunlight at dawn.
So open the windows, let the curtains be drawn.
Then slowly the feet and the hands start to chill,
Though the sun still gleams on the bleak winter hill.
A first promise, of early spring, this could mean,
But for those in the bus queue, no such a dream.
Shivering and shuffling, their purpled faces glow,
For despite the blue sky, they are talking of snow.
How crazy to think, this short burst of sun,
Is but a brief break, before spring is begun,
And this wintry season, has still time to go,
With more icy winds, that are certain to blow.
But this day, my love, gave a pledge of that clear sky,
Where warm, in the sweet, summer grass, we shall lie.

Folkestone, January 1988

MARCH DAFFODILS

Daffodils, now along the Leas
Looking over the March seas.
Yellow trumpets loom in gardens,
Where the frost no longer hardens.
Daffodils in the green spaces,
Lighting up our sallow faces.

Floral harbingers of a new spring,
What a feast of colour you bring,
After the greyness of our winter,
Fog, snow, rain and wind so bitter.

The sun shines over the sparkling waves,
Brightens the bandstand and even saves
Something for the hills, fields and trees
The pavements, houses and people it frees.
Sun, giver of all our life and energy,
Spring resurrection in full majesty.

So sweet is the balm of my love's arms,
Still now is the clangour of alarms
And like the passionate poetry of spring
Fresh light and life to me you'll bring.
Then a loving litany of verse will flow from me
And with such a healing force be borne to thee
Finally, after my struggles, I can let go
Then a calmer, crystal stream will flow.

Folkestone, March 1989

THE HYTHE CANAL

The limpid waters of the canal reflect
The rushes, reeds, the trees, the hill and sky,
Cutting from Hythe to Appledore direct.
South to the sea, the lush Romney marshes lie
And northward the soft escarpment stands
Flecked with sheep along the grassy down,
Not far from the walls of the Roman lands
Where galleys moored to supply the town.
Stately swans along the surface glide,
Fish break the mirror with soft ripples,
Birds float and sing on the bankside,
Breezes brush its length with stipples.
In all weathers, I have walked your banks,
Seeing nature afresh and giving out thanks.

Folkestone, April 1991

THE CHANNEL FROM THE LEAS

The light stains the sky and the seas
Beneath the wooded slopes of the Leas,
Reflecting the colours of the days.
Summer's orange-red, golden rays,
Purple-pinks of dawn, mauve-red at dusk,
Matching the smells of flowers' warm musk.
Winter's cold and sombre shadows
Touching the dirty, dark green billows.
Occasional sunsets of annealed blue-reds
Or yellow-mauve light over frozen flowerbeds.

But what a joy when the sun shines brightly,
Dancing over the glinting waves so lightly,
Glimmering on the soft coast of France
On which the sunbeams so gently dance.
Spring Daffodils along the Leas, blue sea,
Then Autumn's greener waves we sadly see.
But then the Channel capriciously can change,
When savage winds across the narrow waters rage.
Battering with turbulent and predatory force
Ships in the wind and rain, without remorse.

But we shall not forget the drowsy summer's glide
Moving sweetly across the calm and tranquil tide.
So to our creator who made the sea and glorious sun
From which all things in earth and sea or sky have come
We offer praise and thanks, because of you,
From lowly forms of life we slowly grew
To share the joy of your creation
In wonderment and adoration.

Folkestone 1991

THE DELIGHTS OF RAIN

When we have so much rain,
I long to be in sunny Spain,
Or when we drive through clouds of spray,
With water streaming all along the motorway,
Windscreen wipers almost clogged,
Wet windows, steaming and fogged.
I dream of blue skies and warm sea,
Evenings sultry, balmy and carefree.
But then at night the lashing rain,
Beating against the window pane,
The drenching when you go to shop
Wondering if the rain will ever stop.
Now I long for the feel of the hot sand
The tropical breezes of a southern land.
Then I look at the garden and green fields,
Think of the flowers and crops it yields.
Rolling down land glistening green and white,
And in the cornfields, poppies gleam so bright.
I know this growth could never be,
Without the rains that soak the lea.
But now enough of this incessant rain,
I long for the sun to shine again.
To enjoy the garden, valleys and the hills
Without the winds and damp of summer chills.
So rain, it's time you went away,
Come back on some November day.

Folkestone, June 1991

HAM STREET WOODS

Lift up your gaunt, exulting arms
To the powder blue of the winter sky.
Trees of the wood, sing out your psalms,
As straight or gnarled, softly you sigh,
All swaying gently in the chilly breeze
Dappled sunlight illumines your shades,
Exposing the spiky undergrowth and trees.
Golden, shafted light caresses the glades,
The fretted ferns, branches and stark rushes
With variegated, yellow, orange and red brown
And rustling, falling leaves our faces brushes,
From the fading foliage of your summer gown.
Patiently you wait for the coming of spring
As in your russet mantle, peace you bring.

Folkestone, December 1991

THE WARREN

Greenwood jewel, set in the Folkestone coast,
To creatures, trees and plants a gentle host.
Cradled in the tall, chalk channel cliffs,
Sanctuary for the wild in seasons' shifts.
In autumn, brown bracken, dead leaves, crackling dry
And gaunt, stripped trees, reaching up to a leaden sky.
Changing to strange, shadowy shapes in the mist and fogs,
With frost and snow, whitening the brush and fallen logs.
In spring, myriad flowers and lush trees, vibrant with bird song
Dancing colour clouds of butterflies which over buddleias throng.
Adders hide in the fruity brambles and verdant rushes
And rabbits dart and bob in the green summer's bushes.
When sunlight gleams over the treetops from the sparkling sea
The Warren seems suffused with light, from something heavenly.

Folkestone, February 1992

FIRST PRIMROSES

We trudged the Kentish downs in the mist and rain,
Scant signs of spring in the sodden paths and lane,
The clay on our boots a massy, dragging weight.
Hedges spiky, leafless, sharp in winter's state,
Yet there was bleak beauty in the wintry valley fold,
The air pure, pungent and transcendent in the cold.
Trees skeletal, black against the slate sky overhead,
Colours of chalk, clay, shades of green, brown, red.
Beyond the Elizabethan grace of Tappington Hall
Cars far off flashed by in the tree-lined mall.
Then the Jackdaw Inn welcomed but was declined,
Down in the dell a Church with evergreens lined.
High on the windy ridge we paused there and stood
Gave thanks for the sight of primroses in the wood.

Folkestone, March 1992

MAY TIME IN KENT

If you should walk Kent's countryside in May,
Then be prepared to look, to wonder and to pray.
The massy foliage, burgeoning crops and downland light
Will fill you with transcendent, thankful, rare delight.
The hedgerows splashed with flowers and in variegated green;
Joyful, throatful voice of birds that swoop and sing unseen,
Blossom of white, cream and red that decks the trees
Straddle the hills, cluster in the valleys, line the leas.
The sun radiates on the churches of Elham, Acrise and Postling
With their ancient towers, Saxon windows, walls of ragstone filling.
Later we enter the perfect circle of Brockman's bushes dark,
Then pass the soup-plate tower of Etchinghill, so gaunt and stark.
Only ourselves, the meadows, woods and fields upon this walk,
Away from urban madness, anxious minds and frenzied talk.

Folkestone, June 1992

MARTINDALE

We sat together in the sweet hollow of Martindale,
On a bright, calm warm summer evening.
Around, the serried fells encased us in the vale
The tranquillity celestial in the gloaming.
Here in the valley lies the old church of St. Martin,
Bare stone, stark altar, three Bibles, a simple pew,
Stripped of pretension in the presence of its maker
From whose hands this place of peace and beauty grew.
Fells towered above, green, blue-grey, misty to the sky,
Slate-green slopes, with mottled heather and bright fern.
Woolly flecks of sheep scattered upon the hillside lie.
Images of nature's still centre into the memory burn.
At Ullswater, the boats, hills and trees in shadowy reflection.
Oh foolish modern man, what caused you so to lose your direction?

Folkestone, July 1992

HYTHE CANAL IN AUTUMN

The Hythe canal in autumn is a rare delight,
With weed-free, limpid, burnished face.
The late October days with their mellow light
Caress the eyes, reflecting on the surface.
Trees and shrubs along the banks are glowing
Yellow, orange, rust and scarlet with autumn dye,
Leaves line the tow-path underfoot, crackling.
Trees fretted by gales are stark against the sky,
Evergreens remain to contrast the colours of the day,
Birds still sing and swoop, preparing for winter's test,
The air sweet and clear across the rich marsh way,
The escarpment, dun and green, rises to the Church crest.
All mirrored in the water, beauty, colour, form,
Tranquil in its subtle glory, before the winter storm.

Folkestone, November 1992

WINTER ON THE HYTHE CANAL

Sunlight concertina-like over the shining ice,
Children: Breughel figures on the slippery surface.
Long perspective of the canal held in an icy vice,
Lined with gaunt trees, foliage like black lace.
A few red berries remain in the brittle, brown bushes,
Footprints in the frozen mud like fossils lie.
Frost glistens on the grass and on waterside rushes.
High on the ridge a radio warning disc casts its eye,
The ochre light illuminates the green-brown hill
Where huddled white woolly shapes of sheep
Gather in the lower folds, silent and still.
Water, hills and marsh deep in winter's sleep.
The dull yellow sun plate, turns annealed red and gleams
Through the leafless branches, with its penultimate beams.

Folkestone, January 1993

SNOWDROPS

An unseasonable, warm, early March day,
Dun-coloured fields under blue skies around Saltwood,
Then into Brockhill Park we made our way.
There at the edge of the copse they all stood,
A white carpet of snowdrops gleaming
By the stream side, shining and serene,
Through the bare branches sunlight beaming.
For tired, winter eyes a gladsome scene.
We sought to capture the miracle on camera
Knowing it would be just a fragment
Of the enchanted, dappled, woodland panorama,
But memory would fix this small firmament
Recalling the vision of nature's annual rebirth,
The divine resurrection of life upon this earth.

Folkestone, March 1993

KEARSNEY

God is in all the Universe, seen or unseen,
But in the stillness of nature's tranquil beauty
His presence dwells all-powerful and serene,
And at Kearsney Manor He reigns in quiet glory.
The white timbered house, reflected in the lake,
Stream fed, with leaping trout over clear stones,
Ducks, moorhens, swans with cygnets in their wake,
Shades of green, copper foliage in spring's tones.
Glimpse of meadow and woods beyond
The perimeter hedge of thorn and wild flowers
Nettles, toadstools, cow parsley and frond.
Ivy-encrusted trees, tall in the still bowers.
Little is said, much is given and received,
Then later, as for our Saviour we grieved,
Reflected on our lives, sins, opportunities missed
Were forgiven, healed, strengthened by the Eucharist.

Folkestone, May 1993

MOON RISE

The summer sun sets, staining the sea and sky
Outlining the squat towers of the Dungeness station
And softly glows behind the roofs of Hythe nearby.
The horizon, mauve, pink, yellow in subtle variation.
Along the shore, the outgoing tide leaves the lagoons
While the near-still sea mirrors the fading sunset.
Over the angular, dark, green breakwater are festoons
Of seaweed, cordage and tendrils of torn fishing nets.
Turning back to Sandgate, the new moon, silver grey
Emerges slowly to full radiance in the gloaming
As bright across the rippled surface stream the rays,
Casting from a celestial silver disc its gleaming.
Through moonbeams reflected in the sea, glides a skiff.
Glorious late August eve, the beauty of nature's gift.

Folkestone, August 1993

AUTUMNAL IMAGES

Oh tender, sweet, sad autumn, that brings with you,
The mist, the rain, cool winds and skies of pallid blue.
Calm seas that change to grey-green tumult overnight.
Trees and bushes that change their livery in the mellow light
To yellow, orange, red, brown, in bright or subtle toned array,
With seasonal smells of fruitfulness or cloying, damp decay.
In woods, parks and fields, the birds still sweetly sing,
But of the still, warm south, to where they soon will wing.
Bristling stubble stands, besides the sprouting winter greens
And gulls pursue the plough, diving with harsh, greedy screams.
Digging, clearing, pruning we make the garden stripped and stark,
With scent of woodsmoke, red glow of burning leaves in the dark.
In hedgerows, berries and nuts are offered up for us to gather.
Shops display the harvest colours, all neatly stacked together.
In classrooms and campuses, new friends and knowledge to attain
And city lights in the early dusk, tempt their patrons out again.

Folkestone, October 1993

ANTHEM TO LAKELAND

Sing praise and thanks to the Creator of the Universe
For the divine gift of our English Lakeland.
Such skies painted with changing, subtle hues diverse,
Framing the forests, fells and lakes with heavenly hand.
Meadows and hillsides decked in flowers and heather,
Sheep browse and sleep in bracken and on pasture green.
Buttermere, Windermere, Ennerdale with shimmering water,
Reflecting the woods, valleys and the peaks serene.
Clear sparkling streams tumble over the mountainside,
Eskdale, lined with sycamore, ash, oak and alder,
Rowan, silver birch where the summer birds sing and hide.
Cool, crystal rivers coursing over bright stones and boulder.
Symphony of sights, scents and nature's healing sounds,
Restoring, calming, healing the stress of all our wounds.

July 1994

HARVEST TIME IN TEMPLE EWELL

We climbed through the small, shady wood
Out onto the bright chalky slopes of Temple Ewell.
There, feasted on the vista of the rich rolling vale,
Felt the hot sun and gentle breeze, then stood
Transcendent in the beauty of the glorious downs.
Blue sky vaulting the patchwork of stubble and field,
Drums of straw, the residue from the harvest's yield.
Hedgerow, copse, hill and meadow in late summer gowns,
Season of apples, pears, nuts and berries on laden tree,
Waving ripe red corn, still waiting for the reaper's hand.
Fruit of man's labour and God's own bounteous land.
Birds sing and insects hum; a kestrel floats, majestic, free.
Myriad butterflies flit among the bright wild flowers,
Here we can worship, away from city streets and towers.

August 1994

SNOW STORM

The squall blew along the wind swept Leas
Buffeting and freezing from the wintry seas
But the sky overhead was a powdery blue
Then slowly it changed to a strange orange hue,
Dissolving to ochre and thence to a sooty grey
Storm clouds drawing the dark curtain of the day.
Then the light faded into foreboding gloom
Shrouding the shore with apocalyptic doom.
The gale slackened in the early stricken night,
Came the first snowflakes, with face-needling flight,
Covering my cap and coat with a cold white skin
Settling cold and moist on my lips, as I licked them in.
Struggled half-blind through the blizzard to my home
Back to warmth and light, it was not a night to roam.

March 1995

SUMMER EVENINGS

When winter grips the Folkestone Leas,
With rain and snow in a bitter icy freeze,
I think of the warm and gentle breeze
Of summer that caresses the narrow seas,
Where the cliffs of France so clearly stand
And the sun shines bright on the Gallic strand.

The band has ceased to play at last
The listeners and dancers homeward passed,
But an air of pleasure and of ease
Pervades the grass, the blossom and trees.
Then the summer evening starts to descend
And the sound of bird songs sweetly blends.
The still warm earth lies under the feet,
Old folk and lovers lounge in the vacant seats.

The fragrance of foliage, plants and flowers
Is borne on the soft wind from a recent shower
And over the sea, soft ripples glide
With sunlight sparkling over the placid tide,
Slowly the colours change over the darkening sky
And the red disc of the sun slips away with a sigh.
In the dark, blue vault above can be seen
The moon and stars with their silver sheen.

June 1995

DUNGENESS

Take the light railway from Hythe to Dungeness
Preferably on some fine summer's day,
With a pungent smell of steam in your nostrils
Crouched in the toy, cramped carriages,
Passengers merry, in the warm sunshine.
Soon the villas and bungalows slip away,
Skirting the calm, bottle green waters of the canal,
Then passing the lush meadows and fields heavy with harvest,
All the reclaimed richness of Romney marsh, level to the horizon.
Hooting over dykes, past startled sheep and cattle
Past strips of housing at Dymchurch and New Romney,
Passing the sands of Littlestone and Greatstone
To the great banks of shingle of Dungeness.
Here the gaunt citadel of the Nuclear Power station
Dominates the scene like a dreaming monster
With occasional steam snorting from its vents.
Nearby is the old lighthouse, relic of another age.
Brightly coloured fishing boats lie beached on the stony strand,
Myriad birds wheel with songs and cries in different cadences.
Curlew, Sanderling, Turnstone and many species of sea gull.
Strange, exotic plants and flowers burst up through the pebbles
Oat grass, Sea Kale, Vipers Bugloss, Yellow horned poppy.
Among the shingly dunes, lie shacks for fishing and living,
Scattered forlornly among the pebbly wasteland,
Like clapboard structures from a deserted Western movie set.
Humans are dwarfed by the great expanse of sea and sky
Of this immense panorama at the end of the line.

Folkestone, July 1995

ORCHIDS ON THE FOLKESTONE DOWNS

We met on Caesar's camp hillside, the green reservoir below,
The desecrated valley of the Tunnel's blight well in view.
Turning our backs upon it, but not the roar of traffic flow
We went to find the plants, flowers and orchids that here grow.
Then through the woods over Round Hill, where we all stood
At the pilgrims' Holywell, to admire the yellow flags bright.
Did the pilgrims see the poppies scarlet as Christ's blood?
Passing through a marshy valley, we saw the Bee Orchid white,
Then started the ascent of Sugar Loaf Hill, thirsty and hot.
Looking below we saw miniature dogs and walkers by the pond.
Breathless at the top, we sat by the Good Friday crosses spot.
In the descent we paused to admire the Spider Orchid's frond.
Tired but joyful, we walked through blanched fields of Ox-eye daisies,
Mauve-blue Flax and Coltsfoot; blessed nature that the spirit raises.

Folkestone, June 1997

THE COLOURS OF WINTER

When autumn fades and winter seems so cruelly set
And the long, dark nights stretch out ahead,
There is still much colour left in nature's palette –
Stark branches, black, brown, green ochre and red
Variegated shades of evergreen, some with berries bright,
Parks, fields and garden, stark and exposed.
Subtle greens, brown, buff, copper in the colder light,
Frost on hedges, snow over a landscape icily gripped.
The sea, the waves and lakes reflect the changing sky.
But still bloom japonica, jasmine, mahonia, snowdrops.
The contours of the land offer new patterns to the eyes,
And the songs of seasonal birds but rarely stops.
So in its winter vestments nature still gives us pleasure
While waiting for spring to bring us new, wondrous treasures.

Folkestone, February 1998

BLUEBELLS IN REINDEN WOOD

Sunlight's beams shaft into Reinden Wood
Illuminating the glades with their carpets of flowers,
Clusters of bright bluebells sharp against the trees
Enchanted clearings made vibrant by nature's palette,
Refreshing and calming the spirit, gladdening the eye
Storing up images of summer against grey, winter days.
The woodland forms a backcloth of Oak, Larch, Maple,
Willow, Scots Pine, Sweet Chestnut and Silver Birch.
Chrome-yellow clumps of gorse blaze in the foliage.
There scattered in the grasses, ferns and bushes
A profusion of wild flowers, Celandine, Wood anemone,
Herb Paris, Archangel, Purple Orchids, Speedwell and others,
A chromatic display proud in their new livery.
The whole woodland is bursting with the magic of May.
Sweet and pungent odours arise from soil and flora
And the songs of many birds resound from the treetops.
This ancient wood, recorded in the Doomsday Book,
Is still here despite man's greed and many wars –
Some evidence that still remains in the undergrowth.
But the plenitude and beauty of nature still bursts forth
Again at this early summer season, Thanks be to God.

Folkestone, May 1999

ICKWELL BURY

Blessed Ickwell Bury, what peace you always bring,
With fields and copses and where sweet birds sing.
Set in rural comeliness and near the village green,
Your courtyard welcomes, under Tompion's clock serene.
Horses browse in the nearby quiet, verdant pastures
And the ancient redbrick wall your lovely garden nurtures,
Diffusing on flowers, fruit and vegetables a special light.
The passing clouds, dawn, dusk, moonlight or noon-day bright
Are reflected in your still lake, with its mysterious sheen
Here swans, ducks, moorhens, even herons can be seen.
Trees, bushes and rushes are also mirrored in its surface,
The very fabric and people of the Bury seem to give it grace.
Yet it is not only in the beauty of this place so plain to see
But also something timeless, tranquil, with love's healing energy.

July 1999

THE QUIET DAY

The spirit moves across the limpid lake,
It's in the reflection of the sky, the trees and bushes,
The flowers, the grass, the calls the moorhens make,
It's in the fishes, the small waterfall and rushes.
All these things proclaim your love for us,
Offering peace, inner stillness and tranquillity
Away from life's anxiety, its fret and fuss.
Giving us time to reflect upon our own true destiny,
Calm in your presence in this holy, blessed place,
Imbuing us with strength, courage, and with healing
And a needful time to thank you for your grace.
Waiting on you here at Kearsney, By Christ's heeding.
So now we give you thanks and praise for being here
To share with us the Eucharist, in memory of your Son so dear.

Kearsney, Dover, September 1999

IT'S A DOG'S LIFE

Dennis and Stella at Sheffield Park, August 1997

Sparky on Folkestone beach

DOGGEREL

For three times each and every day
Purds must surely have her way.
Walkies usually in the park
Even when it's wet and dark.
Winter, summer, autumn and spring,
Out to the wood and grass we bring
Her for her daily poos and pees
All among the shrubs and trees,
But for social reasons sound
This must be picked up from the ground
So plastic bags we need to carry
To face the daily natural sally.
Not only for these basic reasons
Must she be run throughout the seasons,
Purds loves to sniff exciting things
Who knows what canine bliss it brings.
She loves the forest and the Leas,
The sea, the fields, the Warren's breeze
That brightens up her glossy coat
And fluffs up her white and brindle throat.
Spoiled she is with cuddles and strokes
Milk and treats from sundry folks,
She has a character that's quite unique
And rarely gets a fit of pique.
We love her still, despite her smelly face
And the piles of hair she leaves around the place.

Folkestone, April 1993

WORDS FOR PURDS

We have an old dog called Purdy
Who was once fit, agile and sturdy
Now, aged 12, she sleeps quite a deal,
and usually snores, after a meal.
Dreaming of walks to the Warren or Leas,
Then grunts to wake up and scratch the fleas.
Drifts off again to chase rabbit and cats,
Perhaps the ducks or even large rats.
Wakes up to give her coat a good lick,
Barks when she sees her lead and my stick.
Knows a few words like "Walkies" and "Box",
But more like "Bunce", the cunning old fox.
Each night when her drink of milk is due,
She is restless and vocal, almost on cue.
Her coat has still a soft, velvety sheen –
Alas, hairs abound where she's just been,
And cursing is heard when the vacuum's out
Which she hates, and hides her greying snout.
But when she jumps up to lie on my lap,
For the fleas and stink, I don't give a rap.
She soothes me with her cold, gentle muzzle,
And cuddling her, I don't find it a puzzle,
That this smelly old dog, with her silly grin,
Has taken her softy old stepfather in.

Folkestone, January 1994

PURDS AS PENSIONER

I'm getting old and find it hard to run
And my arthritis makes the stairs no fun,
So I often lie down to bask in the fitful sun
For lately my walks are soon over and done,
Just for the basic functions you understand
In some nearby park or convenient wasteland.
My once strong, white teeth are going home at last
Sadly they're a bit smelly and more in yellow cast.
But each day I roam in my sleep with quiet zest
To places in the woods, or seashore we knew best
And I grunt, snore and bark in my restless dreams
Of the rambles, beef bones and the tasty ice creams,
You gave me sometimes along the bright summer Leas,
Then the sniffing and chasing among the Warren trees.
But my ears and soft coat you still like to stroke
Even if as a fierce guard dog, I'm just a joke.
I love you and miss you whenever you're out
And when you go on hols, I really feel the clout,
But I know you'll be good to me as long as I'm here,
So when I die, bury me in Lyminge Forest, I love so dear.

Folkestone, July 1995

LEADER OF THE PACK

We shall never forget that cold autumn day
Around Lyminge, with the White Cliffs walkers.
'Dogs on leads' they said, but then relented.
So off you raced, leader of the pack, old Purds.
Over the fields, along the deep muddy tracks,
Through the stiles and orange-red copses.
All the afternoon, up front, then into the early dusk,
Later begging for a piece of cake in the village square.
Then only a year later came the decline.
Blind, deaf, arthritic, cancerous, breathless and smelly
Your poor decayed teeth contained only by drugs,
Desperate for food because of the steroids,
Whining at dawn for your meat and biscuit.
Walk-shy now, snoring with air-gulping noises.
Your lovable, smiling tongue, laughing personality gone.

So it was time to say farewell.
Would that we all go so peacefully and painlessly –
The gentle vet carefully pushed the syringe
With its cobalt-coloured anaesthetic
Into your shaven foreleg and you passed away.
We may not regret the bitter cold, daybreak walks
Because of your incontinence,
But have missed your healing doggy presence,
Your excited greetings when we came in;
Your squeaks when you saw rucksacks and sticks,
Your brindle coat and velvety ears.
Memories remain of you over sands, fields and woods,
Barking at the ducks on the park ponds,

The games you liked to play with ring and ball,
Evening on the settee with you across my chest,
Your love of ice cream on the Leas in summer.
Sleep peacefully in your canine heaven our beloved Purds,
You were dearer and nearer to us.
Than any prize winning Crufts thoroughbred.

April 1996

SPARKY

At the Rescue Centre, you sat in the end cage
Next to the large dogs barking in anxiety and rage.
Abandoned creatures, confused by their rejection,
Frantic with fear, but still noisy in their dejection.
But you were quiet, accepting of your sad fate
What, who, why had produced your present sorry state?
We took you for a walk in the warm spring sunshine,
Your game, slender body seemed pared down fine
But you were bouncy, comical and with a questing smile
Moving as if on springs, as we walked about a mile.
You glowed with affection and a strange awareness
Sparkling with energy and a certain joyousness.
So we named you Sparky, such a name it had to be,
And agreed to take you, care for you and set you free.
We had to leave the other dogs, distraught in their cages
But the Centre tries to house them, at some later stages.
Of course a small, white mongrel of unknown terrier breed
Would never at Crufts, be permitted to proceed.
You snuggled up against me as we left the Centre,
To leave trauma behind, for some new loving venture.
And now dear little Sparky you are part of the family
Charming children and adults as you trot out on your 'Walkie'.

Folkestone, September 1998

SPARKY'S WALKIES

Little Sparky Hawes
Comes back with muddy paws
From running in the park,
Racing and wheeling with his funny bark –
For him, it's all a jolly lark.
Then he stops to make his marker pee
And sniff each post, bush and base of tree.
His face is all wreathed in doggy smiles,
You know he could run for miles and miles.
Such happiness upon his face is plain to see
And if his friends are there, it's extra glee.
To see him gambolling and trotting so carefree,
Makes Sparky's presence such a joy for you and me.

November 1999

SPARKY'S TOYS

Sparky has now acquired a cache of toys
Which seem to bring to him doggy joys.
Growling, chewing, displaying his terrier genes
And inviting us to share his crazy canine schemes.
But beware because he wants to play
His sports most every night and day.
Ball, socks, hedgehog and rabbit too
Kong, plastic shoe and his beloved teddy true.
But of all the things he loves by far the most
Is my old gnawed slipper, only just a ghost
Of its former glory, now so tattered and forlorn,
And without care the new ones could soon be torn.
For to keep my toes intact is no mean feat
As he believes my feet are just another treat!
But all this play which seems so new to him
Must help him forget his previous life so grim,
And his charm, affection and his love of fun
Ensures each day our hearts are newly won.

Folkestone, November 1999

REFLECTIONS

Above: Reconciliation: Ivy with her great friend, Gisela, from Cologne, Germany

Left: Easter at Kearsney Abbey

WAS THERE A RESURRECTION?

Was there a resurrection on that far off Easter morn,
That followed a cruel crucifixion on some desolate hill?
And did his mother come to the cavern at dawn to mourn,
Weeping with frosted tears upon the sunrise chill?
And were angels watching the place where he had lain?
While with his friends unknown along the dusty track he trod,
At last to stand before them unknown, all knowing without pain,
Revealed at last to all mankind, the own true son of God.
And did he really give them broiled fish with pierced hands,
From whence they knew the world must needs be fed
By them bearing the precious food to distant lands,
Through other calvaries, to lead and to be led?
Yes, it all was so, for by the gospels and our faith we know,
Life brings many crucifixions, resurrections and by this we grow.

Folkestone, April 1986

QUESTIONS OF FAITH

Lord I have a problem with some aspects of Christian doctrine,
Like our Saviour's divinity and his place in space and time?
Then the question of virgin birth, so alien to the scientific mind,
Presents some difficult genetic questions to the modern mind I find?
The Crucifixion, Resurrection, also for a computer age seem odd,
Questioning this could happen to the son of our creation's God?
Then the matter of the Eucharist, the blessing of bread and wine,
Can it bring forgiveness and healing by some great power Divine?
How about God's will, free will, sin, Satan, Heaven and Hell.
Is this all to be accepted, together with archangels as well?
Then a God of love, with evil, earthquake, famine, sickness and pain,
That throughout the ages and still upon the earth today remain?
And the writing of the Bible, so scrutinised by some today,
With dates, places, persons, often historically suspect they say?
Or the endless sermons and debates about the Holy Trinity
With arguments often beyond the average man's ability?

So Lord teach us to pray with love, faith and true humility
Waiting in stillness for the answers that will come eventually.
For certainly we know that Christ's words can be the only creed
To check the selfishness, the folly and the drive of human greed.
Goodness, truth and beauty are part of the Christian goal,
Bringing fulfilment and healing to each body, mind and soul.
This message of love and service given by Christ with such authority,
Could only come from a sacred source, inspired by true divinity.
Thus strengthened by his example and living the word each day,
We may by faith, hope and love, bring all people to walk this way.
Then all creation, by your grace will come to its perfection
And each person enter the kingdom, by Christ's resurrection.

Folkestone, June 1997

RETREAT

I look to the stubby hills above this town
They fill me with grace I've rarely known.
My brow no longer cracks with anxious frown
I dare not think, of that from which I've flown.
For now at last I've found some fragile peace
From years of working fears, lies and deceit,
In cities where the dirt and traffic never cease
Whose crowded, concrete campments cry defeat.
Here once, the sweet communion of our youthful souls,
Our bodies, friendships, dreams and hopes so dear
Crashed gratingly to earth like precious porcelain bowls
And all became a zone of ever darkening fear.
Yet in this place where hills and sea lie gently cast
We may in time, in part, recover fragments from the past.

Folkestone, February 1986

RETIREMENT

He sits writing in the public library
Under the bust of William Harvey
Waiting for inspiration to produce some verse,
But sadly each stanza just gets steadily worse.
January afternoon, dreary, dark, cold, rainy,
Hardly the time for being bright or brainy.
Retired librarian, still in a familiar location,
Having difficulty in handling his new vocation.
Leisure to be a great challenge to his skill,
Poems, paintings, nature, study all to fulfil,
But winter has stunted his aspiration
Age diminished his energy and perception.
Sleeps badly, is scared of all manner of things
Is fearful of the comforts that modern life brings.
Central heating, washing machine, even the fridge
Are seen as High Tech problems he now has to bridge.
Lies in bed imagining all kinds of disaster,
Wakes anxious, trembling, his heart racing faster.
Kills time in the shops, the Legion, the swimming pool,
Trying to save cash on his central heating, old fool.
Sensible Pensioners should fly off to the sun,
For then winter in retirement might well be fun.

Folkestone, January 1989

THE POISONED POND

Early morning with bright, sharp sunshine,
Dull sheen on the limpid pond,
Scummy froth around the garbage at the edges.
Hard reflections of blue sky, trees and rushes,
Subtle shades of blues and greens
All heralding a warm perfect summer day.

But the exposed banks of the pond,
Dry concrete and clay
Are like the exposed gums of a geriatric
And sinister silver flecks lie motionless
In the dark, green, viscous water.
Others still struggle for life and air,
Dulled eyes, gasping fish mouths
Breaking the surface, sucking with desperation.
No other sound in the still, summer morning.

Then splashing and squelching of anglers,
Cries of anger as they collect the dead fish.
Gudgeon, bream, tench, majestic carp
Are laid in serried ranks.
Silver, aluminium and gold-bronze scales glinting
Then fast dulling in the warm air.
Corpses stuffed into municipal garbage bins,
Ignominious cadavers, protruding heads and tails
Fast rotting in the hot summer sun.
Victims of bureaucracy and selfishness.
Shall we all be gasping for air one day?

Folkestone, July 1990

THE BETRAYAL

I threw a crust of bread away today
Couldn't be bothered to feed the birds.
then thought of those mountains grey
Where the frozen and famished Kurds,
Were dying in the freezing mud
Fighting for fragments of bread
Some with wounds seeping blood
Barefoot in the snow they fled,
From the face of bloody repression.
The allies called on them to rise
Shake off sadist Saddam's oppression.
Was it US cynicism or simply lies?
For no Bill of Rights or Habeas Corpus,
Was served upon those Kurdish corpses.

Folkestone, April 1991

SENSES

From birth to death we receive the material for perception
Soft milky breasts, sounds of disapproval or affirmation.
Taste, touch, visual olfactory and aural codes
Building up the pattern of psyche on life's roads.

Echoes of gentle or harsh voices, traffic and the subway roar,
Smell of the new-mown grass, birds that over mountains soar.
Fish and chips, barbecues, boiled cabbage and the Sunday roast,
Fresh baked bread, fragrant coffee, sight of the Dover coast.

Cool foam and hops on the tongue after a dusty hike,
Cold wind on the face, riding your first adult bike.
Beating of spring and winter rain upon the window pane,
Cold-nostrilled fog, farmyard smell in the country lane.

Bird tracks in the dazzling unmarked snow,
Smell of the classroom when hours are slow.
Battlefield stench, burning tanks, shattered minds and bodies,
Sweat, shit, fear, thirst, the wild ecstasy of liberated cities.

Mozart and Beethoven floating out in a celestial night,
Jazz on a balmy, summer's eve by glittering starlight.
Tang of pines and spicy herbs under an Italian sun,
Caress of a warm, clear sea and the first ski run.

Cicadas, the smell of woodsmoke in the forest glade,
Sunrises and the glorious sunsets that slowly fade.
Touch of lips and fingers on the form of one you love,
The joy of consummation, that passion needs to prove.

Touch-down and take-off as the plane is airborne,
Smell of engine oil and cooking in a squall.
Scent of May blossom, harmony with the Universe,
Sad, grey, wet days, when life seems in reverse.

Gloom after a bitter quarrel's ranting,
The joy of reunion after a sad parting.
Christmas morning with all its childlike magic,
Stained glass, Easter Day, with praise and music.

The richness or poverty that our short lives records,
The quality and variety of all these senses stored,
These myriad, sensory imprints that sadden or delight
Will one day fade away, with the passing of our light.

Folkestone, October 1991

CHRISTMAS

Was there a bright new star, gleaming in the night's blue vault,
Moving, scintillating, to settle over a stable in Bethlehem?
And journeying through the deserts, did Magi come, wise and taut,
Bearing the gifts of gold, frankincense and myrrh with them?
And did the Angelic host burst through the floor of heaven with light?
Filling the simple shepherds on the slopes with awe and mystery,
Casting enchanted sound and radiance, over cold Judean hills of night?
And did they all come to the manger, to worship and to glorify?
We know for sure there was a Roman census at that time decreed.
Nor yet the first, or last, sad record of man's death and birth,
Or marriage, sickness, poverty, wealth, different faith or creed.
Who can say how much of the wonderful Christmas story is true:
We can only say Christ's message of love came thence to me and you.

THAMES TRIP

Take the summer boat from Westminster Pier,
Beside the Thames, Big Ben glows with a golden light,
The Abbey and Parliament are majestic and near,
County Hall and Hungerford Bridge pass in our flight.
Elegant Festival Hall and its shabbier acolytes to art
And soon under Waterloo Bridge we quickly steam.
Then beneath London Bridge and into the City's heart –
But sadly only a glimpse of St. Paul's is seen.
Victorian warehouses and the endless Cubist blocks,
Relieved by glory of Tower Bridge in iron cast,
The massive Tower of London with dungeons and stocks.
Belfast, Cutty Sark and Greenwich Palace are past.
Finally we stop at the aluminium helmets of the Barrage –
What a feast of London, past and present, lies in this passage.

Folkestone, May 1992

RIO SUMMIT

They're flying down to Rio for a summit on pollution,
Before long-suffered nature offers us a final solution,
But the USA carries on with its consumer and production binge.
For such things mainly concern the lunatic, green fringe
And to talk of the energy-guzzling American economy
Is only a case of the moaning Third World perfidy,
Who play the card about our failing planet's health
As crafty ruse to get the USA's wealth by stealth.
Who cares if we blight the land, the air, the sea,
So long as there are plenty of luxuries for a spree.
Things will need to get very much worse we fear,
With disaster and death a great deal more near,
And closer draws near the apocalyptic catastrophe,
While we hesitate, prevaricate and just wait and see.
Now the Communist dream goes up in polluted smoke
And the factories of capitalism are hardly a joke.
The third world sinks in poverty and overpopulation,
Submerged in debt, corruption and savage exploitation.
But sustainable growth with our planet turning green
Must be our urgent goal, not just an idealist's dream.
As the stewards of our Lord's creation
We have failed in almost every nation.
And the words of Christ, to share all in his name
Must be followed, if all is not lost in our shame.

Folkestone, June 1992

THE SEVEN DEADLY SINS

These then are the deadly seven
We need to curb to get to heaven.
The first sin is that of pride
Which puts us on the sinful slide.
The second is that of wrath
An uncontrolled demonic broth.
The third sin is that of envy
Curdling the soul to acidity.
The fourth sin is that of lust
When it's either sex or bust.
The fifth sin is that of avarice
This is surely the Devil's kiss.
The sixth sin is that of gluttony
Swilling and stuffing compulsively.
The seventh sin is that of sloth
When from work the person is loath.
But the sin that causes most distress
Is the thoughtless sin of selfishness.

Folkestone, July 1992

DREAMS

Our dreams are synthesised from many things:
In youth, of love, success and urgent sexuality;
Sweet and sour frames of fantasies that night brings,
Suspended in space and time with stark, unreal clarity.
In middle age, anxieties of work and play
Are re-enacted in scenes symbolic or revealing,
Recording the triumphs and disasters of the day,
Re-run dramas and farces, haunting, soft or searing.
In age, a life-stocked memory now offers a selection,
Drawn from life's failures, deaths and sundry treacheries,
Mixed with travels to paradise or trips to dereliction,
Nocturnal transports filled with joyful or fearful reveries.
But how blessed the conscience that brings each tender night
Sweet unremembered dreams that put all cares to flight.

Folkestone, September 1992

THE EUCHARIST

At the Eucharist, the sacrifice
Of Christ is by us remembered –
Recalling the last supper and the price
He paid for all our sins unnumbered.
And those words in the upper chamber,
Which He spoke that we must cherish,
His love and ministry here together
Lest we should all in darkness perish.
Take, eat my body for you and all mankind,
Drink my blood so precious in this wine.
Such healing and mystic energy we find
In these sacred elements, so holy and divine.
So humbly we kneel down to receive the Host
In the presence of Father, Son and Holy Ghost.

Folkestone, December 1992

GREECE

Hellas what rare gifts to us you brought,
Grace, harmony of body, mind and spirit.
Philosophy, architecture, sculpture finely wrought,
Drama, science, the democracy that we inherit.
Yet still the magic of Cape Sunion glows
And the golden light touches the Parthenon,
Despite the traffic that endlessly flows.
With sapphire seas to swim or meditate upon,
Delphi, where the sacred spirit still remains
And Marathon, Corinth, Epidaurus, Mycenae.
Majestic mountains, flowering spring plains
Jewelled islands remote from modern frenzy.
Sunset still stains your wine dark sea
Father Poseidon, guard this our patrimony.

Folkestone, December 1992

HAPPINESS

Is it?
Contentment and harmony with everyday life?
An exquisite sense of human pleasure and satisfaction?
A transcendent state of cosmic knowing and unknowing?

Does it need?
A secure, loving and stable childhood?
Good health in youth and age?
Confidence of body, mind and spirit?
A unique sense of identity without selfishness?
Freedom from anxiety, guilt and fear?
An ability to make and maintain good relationships?
Equal sharing of body and soul with a loving partner?
An imaginative, intelligent education
Which brings a life-long quest for knowledge?
Skills with tools, crafts and practical matters?
Love of nature in its beauty and structure?
Creativity in science, art and literature?
Appreciation of music, sport and dancing?
Excellent food in excellent company?
Living a life of moderation
Pursuing the good, true and beautiful?

Alas, fate is arbitrary in bestowing its gifts
We may need to settle for less.
And anyway, all these attributes without
Discipline and service to man will not prosper.
We could look to philosophy, religion or politics.
Or is it best to seek and love God, caring for

Our families, community, country and all creation
And to wait for grace?

February 1993

WHOLENESS

Father, I shall strive to be still
Please heal me fully if you will,
I'll listen to your voice in prayer
Firm in the faith of your loving care.
Banish the pain, the hurt, the strife
Lord come into my damaged life.
Jesus, you suffered sore upon the cross
Knowing the torment, loneliness and loss,
Hold my hand now in this darkness
Bring me in your time to gladness,
But above all, I know your will be done
In earth and heaven, together with your Son.
So I place my life into your trust,
That when I die, as die I must,
Forgiven, ransomed, by love and grace
That in true Holiness, I'll find my place.

Folkestone, September 1992

BORROWED TIME

Shut in the white clinical walls
Of the small examination room
I lay on the inspection bed.
Looked down at my naked legs,
Only my red striped shirt
A touch of colour in the sterile room.

The specialist came in, tall, well built
With a red brown moustache,
My life notes in his hand.
"Waterworks OK, a good flow?"
Then he frowned, "I have bad news,
When we did the operation, we found cancer,
Sorry there is no form of treatment,
A year or three perhaps to live.
So live it to the full, old chap,
Come back and see me in three months."
He answered my few fearful questions and left.

My bare legs and feet trembled.
I struggled into my clothes,
Stumbled out into the weak March sunlight.
What now, where will the future pain erupt?
What degradation of terminal illness, suicide?
Tubed up, wired up, waiting for a Hospice?
How can I tell Stella, family and friends?
What hymns for my funeral?
Got home, took the dog for a walk,
Enjoyed the sun setting over the pond.

Saw plenty of deaths as an infantryman,
Even sometimes wished to die quickly myself,
To blot out the danger, dirt, cold, thirst.
Now it seems it must be faced with certainty.
The borrowed time is being recalled.

Thank you, Lord for giving me such a rich life,
Full of friendships, love, professional success,
Travel, books, art, music, nature and swimming
And for some modest creativity,
Even bringing me back to Christ belatedly.
Now I must prepare myself to meet you,
Believing in your love and forgiveness,
Praying the Holy Spirit will comfort me in my pain
And with faith in the knowledge of Christ's sacrifice,
Trusting you will judge me with mercy
When at last I stand before you.

Folkestone, March 1994

THE CREDIT SIDE OF LIFE

When sometimes life seems heavy and grim
Remember the good times with a grin.
The energy of youth, everything vibrant and new,
Love of parents and family close to you.
Aroma of coffee, bacon and memorable meals,
April's first warmth, spring flowers, church bell peals.
Success at sports, acclaim of your peers
Hot showers with the team, boozy cheers.
Sunlight on water, rivers, lakes and sea
Reflecting the hills, mountains and the lea.
Standing on mountain tops, looking over the vales
With pastures, heather and rocky, ferny dales.

Cold drinks in bars as the red sun stains the waves
Diving in crystal seas to coral depths and caves.
The warmth of the sun, scent of pines and kerosene
After a flight back to a well loved scene.
Lying in someone's arms after lovemaking, sweet and sharing
With a lover of understanding, passionate, lovely, caring.
Greek temples in the honey light of the afternoon sun
Bookshops and libraries, from where knowledge has come.
Pleasures of theatres, galleries and museums
Places of fantasy, antiquity and visionary dreams.
Heavenly music in some enchanted place
Which made the heart to soar and race.
The post with good news, cheques and exams passed
Satisfaction of academic and job effort rewarded.
The magic of childhood Christmas with joyful memories;
Cathedral choir singing at solemn services.

Dancing with a partner with rhythm and grace
When you lose all sense of time and space.
The heavy sleep when you've just pulled out of the line
Tea and hot food after lying in a slit trench supine.
Meditation on a warm still, bright summer morn
With renewal of a force, making you feel newborn.
What a feast of experiences it would surely seem
And what a privilege life has largely been.

March 1995

NIGHTLIFE

We are mainly fashioned from our memory –
By day we are mostly in charge of this activity,
But at night we all return to the mind jungle,
Treading its trackways, trying to sort the tangle.
The forgotten, half-forgotten or clear remembrances
Of success, failure, guilt or life's missed chances.
Books, rituals, films, radio, TV programmes we find
Form part of the data, fed into the voracious mind.
Childhood misery, joy, frustrated or fulfilled sex,
Trauma, conflict are all stored in experience index.
At night as passengers in weird arrivals and departures
Crystal or confused glimpses of paradise and hell ensues.
Real, surreal images emerge from the shadowy domain
Where fantastic, convoluted and distorted symbols reign.
Sometimes we are actors, performing on strange stages
On sets or scenes drawn from all our different ages,
Then transported to other lives in time and space.
And when at dawn we once again rejoin the human race,
Information of nocturnal travel mostly sinks without a trace.
They say dreams are nature's way to deeper rest
But nightmares can put this theory to the test.
So when we pass away into life's last, unwakeable sleep
What of the archive of our psyche or dreams shall we keep?

March 1996

CONSOLATIONS OF AGE

Old age should bring peace and tranquillity,
Wisdom, understanding and increasing charity.
Alas too often the worst features of the personality
Can sometimes increase with approaching senility.
But there are many bonuses, like no daily commuting
With uncertain public transport stressful, exhausting.
Then driving through the fog, snow or rain
Is also a daily dose of nervous strain.

In sunshine the OAP can sit under the garden tree
While the worker sweats in the office or factory.
The OAP can take discount holidays at any time or place
But the choice is limited for those in the rat race.
Concessions on travel and many other things,
Chance for dilettantism in the leisure it brings.
Time for all the hobbies of your choice
Letters to the papers, airing your views and voice.
Gentle sports, swimming, golf or bowls
Good for the body, good for the soul.
Sex or siesta in the afternoon
Can also be a daily dream or boon.
Voluntary work or adult education
Can bring much pleasure and satisfaction.

Then all those books you always wanted to read
Will you read them or, just watch TV instead?
These compensations will of course depend
On your health, interests and retirement stipend.
With your past diet, your fondness for booze and fags

The spare parts you need and the belly that sags.
On the traumas of war, redundancy or divorce
The stress of your old job, its nature and course.
To some, loss of power will be a deadly bore
And some workaholics will need to find another chore.
Then don't expect from your kids that you'll be free
Their problems and their kids you'll still have to see.
It all depends on what survives of body, mind and soul
And what still stays intact, as we reach our final goal.
But life is usually sweet, whether in youth or in age
So we'll pray for understanding, both caring and sage.

Folkestone, June 1996

A PRAYER FOR DOCTORS

Lord, be with our doctors in the interval
Before the next patient's, impatient call.
Bring some stillness into their crowded day,
Grant them strength and the right words to say,
So that each patient may be made whole,
Healed in body, mind and soul.
Their packed waiting room seethes with sad people
The young, the old, malingerers and hypochondriacal,
With their smells, their sights, their sighs and noise
All to be treated with professional care and poise.
Our doctors' humanity is so often sorely tested
With too many vital decisions instantly expected.
But a doctor is Christ's hands, eyes, ears and brain,
Consoling Him, as they relieve each person's pain.

July 1997

SILENCE

Silence or solitude is often very hard to find,
Amidst the selfish, restless stress of modern life.
But we need peace and quiet to restore the mind,
Stillness when often the overload is rife.
Sadly for some, silence can increase their isolation,
Bringing anxiety or a sad descent into a dark cage,
For a basic human need is surely that of conversation?
Silence can also be wordless joy, or sullen rage.
In a culture consumed by consumerism, greedy profit,
Frenzied work place, hysteric noise, mass production,
Often denying the growth of body, mind and spirit.
We need to pray, wait and listen in silence for direction –
Great healing and wholeness can come from silent meditation
Finding our true selves, touched by the essence of creation.

Folkestone, February 1998

WHAT ARE WE?

The nature and nurture debate is still quite unresolved
For we carry in our genes so much baggage from the past,
Determining much of the spirit, mind and body to be formed.
Saints, heroes, villains, madmen and many others in the cast.
Even the genes may malfunction, with future problems to unfold.
Poverty, parenting, relationships, boring job, no creative prospects.
All play a part and education is a vital factor in the mould.
Education from nursery to old age, ought to help us to detect
The influence of our debased culture and its media banality
Brainwashing for so many, from the cradle to the grave,
Creating an uncritical, critical mass, unsure of their identity.
The effect of injury, illness, trauma can also the psyche enslave.
So what is left of the free will to create our own personality?
For if we are not puppets, some decisions must shape our destiny?

Folkestone, March 1998

MY LOVE OF SWIMMING

Gibbon wrote 'I would not exchange my invincible love of reading for all the treasures of India.' Amen to that I would say, but would like to insert 'and swimming' after 'reading'.

As a child and even as a young man, I was an indifferent swimmer, having learned in the local Public Baths in the 1930's. The London Borough of Camden is about to close that pool. Tuition was virtually non-existent. Some of the poorer boys, without full-length regulation costume, had to wear loincloths, given out free by the Baths. They were called 'balls cuddlers' by the others. Towels could be hired from the Baths, although few did. This practice stopped in the 1960's because of theft. My own swimming happened, as with so many, mainly by accident: at one time I was clinging to the side, the next moving up lengths with a passable sidestroke. It was enough to save my life on the Normandy landing in 1944, when the tank I was clinging to was let down into deep water.

For a while after the war, dancing and chasing women became the main source of exercise. Then I went to work in a Public Library, which was part of a Municipal block containing a swimming pool. There I became friendly with the Assistant Baths Manager, who had served in another battalion of my Regiment. I often went back to work exhausted or 'Trimmed', Trim being his name. I never looked back from that time. Over the year I acquired breastroke, front crawl, backstroke and some butterfly.

Unless I have been ill I have always managed several swims a week, sometimes twice a day in summer. Even when away on business, I always took my trunks hoping for a swim. I once forfeited the chance of a good position when I hesitated, thinking about the travel problems and how it might prevent my regular swimming.

Soon after I took up swimming, my marriage became difficult and I found great emotional release and I suspect sexual sublimation as well. If I had been an ancient Greek, my God would have been Poseidon. The superb bronze statue of the god was taken out of the sea by fishermen's nets and is now in the National Museum in Athens. I need hardly say, it's one of my favourite bronzes. Poseidon has served me well over the years, but has nearly claimed me a couple of times, due to my arrogance. Once on holiday, I went swimming in a storm with the red flags flying. Swimming on the same spot for an hour and getting no nearer shore can be a terrifying experience. Poseidon spared me and I got through the surf by a miracle. Some of the best swimming and diving is still possible off the Greek Islands, despite the pollution of the Mediterranean.

Sadly, I am negatively buoyant, which means I do not float easily, a great disadvantage to a swimmer. The best swimmers have buoyancy, style and endurance; I had mainly the latter. This heavy weight in the water served me well when I qualified as a sub-aqua diver, and as a snorkeller on holiday, still my favourite vacation. Diving at Eilat in Israel on the coral reef was one of my best holidays. Of course, the holiday in Israel had many other wonderful things to commend it.

So to sum up in praise of swimming: it can be family and friend, or solitary and reflective. At a general level, it does not require a team or specialised equipment, you can even swim in the nude in the right circumstances. It can often be a lifesaver for yourself and others, many people die quite near land and safety because of panic. It is not competitive unless you care to make it so, but all water, particularly the sea, needs to be taken seriously in certain circumstances. It can be addictive but is rarely harmful, being good for the body, mind and spirit; a good lifelong friend that will never let you down.

Since I retired, the local swimming club kindly sent me on an ASA teacher-training course. It taught me a great deal about teaching and improved my own swimming. I have been teaching for six years as a volunteer, trying to put something back into a sport that has given me such health and pleasure. To see the faces of the children and their parents when they are promoted from my class to squad swimming never fails to give me a glow.

So try it, particularly if you can swim and have just not bothered for ages. As you get older it is more difficult to learn but some instructors specialise in this. It is the same with disability – great benefits can accrue for all sorts of problems from Asthma to MS.

Folkestone, May 1992

TREVOR

Trevor, I've found it difficult to write
About our relationship, on this winter's night.
Knowing we loved the warm summer shine,
Blue sky, clear sea, good food and wine.
But, above all, your love of words that sowed
Ideas, ideals, unique thoughts as they flowed
To many people, they so often fired
To radical action, thereby greatly inspired.
What tragic fate deprived you of full speech,
Making it hard to communicate and reach?
This truncation of your gift of verbal usage
You faced with stoic rage and courage.

You came into my life when I carried some baggage,
Newly retired, friendless and with a broken marriage,
They say old friends are the ones loved best
But in the autumn of my life you came with zest,
Showing the meeting of minds, spirit and ideas
Can create a fusion not always brought by years.
We walked the countryside in sun, wind, rain and snow
Like young students with hearts and thoughts aglow,
Hoping for a world where love and justice would reign
And the environment be less ravaged once again.

Your family, who, after the strokes, then served you
With a devotion, loving, practical, faithful and true,
Together with our lovely Rosemary, in every way,
Left little for us to do but to visit and to pray.
So I salute you, my comrade of our war-tried generation,
Who strove so hard to serve man and the Lord's creation.

January 2004

SOCIETY

Left: Taken in Asnelles where 1st Hampshires landed later to take Arromanches

Below: With my Godson, Barnaby, August 2004

O JERUSALEM

O Jerusalem, your scarred, grey walls have seen such bitter pain.
The Holy, golden city on whose fabled streets, thousands have died.
Hebrew, Hoplite, Legionary, Crusader and Saracen in combat slain,
With many innocents, victims of greed or dogma, in the bloody tide.
David, Shepherd, Psalmist, Warrior King, captured your site,
Dancing with joy, then wracked with sorrow by his treacherous kin.
Leaving Solomon to build the glorious city and temple of light,
But misused power, lost faith and wisdom, let the darkness in.
Nobly rebuilt by Herod, temple, palace, towers, streets and wall
Here Jesus taught, was crucified and prophesised your fearful end
By the fury of Rome's might, which wrought your catastrophic fall.
Sadly down the years, the joy of peace did rarely war transcend,
For still today your aged stones resound, with tumult and alarms.
O Jerusalem, when will you fulfil the sacred promise of the psalms?

Folkestone, May 1988

FESTIVAL OF BRITAIN, THE LOST CAUSE

Strolled by the Thames in the summer of '51,
Filled with delight, together with my love,
Dreamed a new age for old Britain had come,
With Skylon, fountains and blue sky above
And graceful domes, pavilions of light.
New industry, agriculture and architecture,
All unfolding to that future bright,
People contented, educated, creative, secure,
Science and art blended to serve humanity
Here at the heart of London's South Bank riverside,
Food for the mind and soul of the city.
Alas now, too few pass the stained walls with pride.
What greed, folly and dogma of political division
Could leave but a shell of that glorious vision.

Folkestone, April 1991

XEROX COPY

John Lennon (God rest his soul) was heard denouncing the evils of bureaucracy, shortly before being murdered by a madman, frequently the fate of prophets. I am not sure if he knew the work of Weber and his followers on the subject, a writer as important as Marx but, alas, not widely read in political circles. John Lennon would have little else in common with Bismarck who said: "The bureaucracy is cancerous in every part of the body. Only the stomach is healthy." This was said about one of the most efficient bureaucracies in the world and it is still serving the German people.

The coming of the computer, systems design and analysis, was going to flush out superfluous staff and streamline management, and, above all, reduce paperwork. This underestimated the power of the bureaucracy. In my lifetime, the size and complexity of the personnel in the public services has grown to alarming proportions. Poor legislation on boundaries, incompetent public auditing and timid ministers in Whitehall have all contributed. It is, however, the power of a bureaucracy to control the means of communication and the flow of information that ensures their growth and survival. It is hardly surprising that politicians often collude with them.

What has this got to do with Xerox copies? I maintain that without ease of photocopying, the bureaucracy might have been contained. Xerox copies are far cheaper for production runs than computer printouts. I worked in one of the older polytechnics for 20 years. In 1960 BX (before Xerox) I would doubt if 250,000 copies were annually generated for academic and administrative use. In 1984 the figure recorded was 8 million, as could be reasonably checked. It was probably nearer 10 million. It need hardly be said that the administrative staff in 1960, amounting to about 10, rose to around 300, not in line with the college growth.

Half a shelf was required to store minutes etc in 1960. By the 1980's it was several shelves. Publications and proceedings of a multitude of committees, working parties, task forces and special teams abounded. Much of this feedstock of bureaucracy was irrelevant. Two or three of the really powerful committees' minutes were all that was necessary to know how the wind was blowing. Sadly much of this redundant material was done in the name of democracy. It is a pity how so many so-called educated people are unaware of the laws of overload and redundancy in information theory.

I must now pause in my diatribe about bureaucracy to confess all. I was a facilitator in this avalanche of paper. It is a modern tale of the sorcerer's apprentice, in which paper takes the place of water. I can only say in my defence that, at the time, I was unaware of the bureaucratic wen that was spreading throughout society.

Being a devotee of the 1960s and a status seeker, I persuaded the Principal of the Polytechnic to purchase one of the first generation of Xerox copiers. In sociological jargon, I sought to increase my centrality (importance or indispensability to the organisation). The previous method of copying journals had been by Photostats (a term that lingered on for years after). Most academics had been content with this in an era of exponential growth in scientific knowledge since 1945. The admin staff were content with the wax stencil or carbons method; the students used the periodicals in the library and there was no mutilation of material in those days. The Principal of the college had left school at 14, studied part-time through 1st and 2nd degrees and a doctorate, and was a leading expert on corrosion, author of books and scientific articles, lay reader and a man with wide interests. They certainly don't make them like that anymore! His interest was mainly scientific, of course, and appeals to this requirement made him agree to my proposed purchase with reservations.

The news of the Xerox installation spread around the Polytechnic like a bush fire in an arid landscape. Within days, admin staff, not only from our own college but also smaller ones in the area, were standing in line. Academic users were rudely elbowed aside and considerable heat was generated, coming not only from the thermal fixer of the machine. It is difficult for a young person today to envisage the heady moment when the first sight of a copy rolled off the machine. It was like being Gutenberg or Fox Talbot without the hard work. It was little wonder that the bureaucrats quickly saw its potential. Even ordinary people could barely resist the fix and subsequent addiction. Everything went on to the platen: learned articles, reports, minutes, letters, specimens from the science departments, theses, football pool coupon, diplomas, personal legal documents, in fact anything remotely 'photocopyable'.

From these modest queues of 1960's were to develop the long, frenzied lines of the 1980's. One of the classic examples of this mania could be seen at the London School of Economics. Here, great crocodiles of students, loaded to hernia point with printed material and visibly clutching £10, £20 and even credit cards, waiting anxiously for the machines. This did not include the huge bank of photocopiers behind the scenes for teaching staff and, no doubt, other departmental ones. The inevitable question must be asked: "How did they manage before photocopying and has it improved efficiency?" The whole area is ripe for serious investigation, both in the private and public sector. I also wondered what Sidney Webb, founder of the LSE, compulsive note-taker and great friend of the old-style Polys, would have made of it? (He was a supporter of the Soviet Union, when it was evident to many that the Russian bureaucracy was oppressing and wrecking the country. It is a safe bet they found the hard currency to buy as many as possible, soon after Xerox put them on the market.)

Within weeks, silence of the Polytechnic library, in which the Xerox was installed, was shattered. There was a clatter of machinery, clink of money, smell of ozone from the UV scanner, panic when it sometimes caught fire. Then the rows and complaints about quality, priority, charges, copyright and understandably frequent breakdown, destroyed all atmosphere of study. The looks of frustration and anxiety on the faces of those denied copying, because of malfunction, defies description. Only Munch has portrayed them.

The Head of Physics Department, whose staff were among some of the justifiable users, came to me with a proposition. He had a friend who would design an air-conditioned, soundproof housing, thus reducing noise and failure rate. The friend duly arrived, made the calculations and submitted the plan, which was passed to administration, where it sank without a trace. It will never be ascertained whether they resented the interference or favoured a contractor friend of the chief administrator. I lean to the latter, as the small bureaucracy of that time were less devious and more transparently corrupt. The contractor arrived, beautifully dressed, "to examine the location", he said. "Don't worry about the plans, it's all in hand". Classic words that had presaged some of his other expensive mistakes in the college. I was not comforted.

During the summer recess, his men arrived and proceed to throw up a hardboards shack around the machine. this was done without benefit of any, in defiance of, any plan. It took no expert on thermodynamics to see the installation had no chance of survival. They had, however, chosen the time when the academics would be away for about ten weeks. The library staff waited anxiously for the next session. Even with the small volume of copying during the vacation, the copier broke down with the heat a coupe of times. As soon as the work accelerated in September, the machine burst in to flames. I briefly enjoyed the drama of extinguishing the flames it with CO_2 cylinder, but strong people were led away weeping, to from the fumes but with frustration.

When the teaching staff returned in force, there was a colossal row. As o disciplinary action was taken against the admin staff, I assumed the academics had been bought off with extra resources or other concessions. Security was tight about the consequences but secretaries spoke of raised voices and red, angry faces coming out of the Principal's office, so the scenes will have to be imagined.

Tentative attempts to improve the Xerox housing was made by

removing the roof and drilling large holes in the side to let air in. Further pathetic efforts were made to stick acoustic tiles inside to reduce sound. The whole ludicrous structure began to look like a dirty Gruyere cheese stockade. Finally, the maintenance staff removed the shambles over a weekend. The Xerox was eventually found a home in an adjacent passage, where it was more used and abused in its new, unsupervised position and copyright became a joke. Monthly returns giving departmental usage created fresh acrimony and cash became a serous security problem.

When we moved to a new building, self-registering keys, photocopying credit cards, numerous machines in academic departments and admin offices seemed to contain the problem. But in my mind's eye, I can still see the anxious faces and hear the angry cries in the passage which led from the eventual Xerox room to my office. Of course the spread of the post war bureaucracy is not seriously to be explained in terms of photocopiers, but what a powerful tool they presented, far more so than the computer, which is often used blindly, without fully understanding its potential.

August 1992

TUNNEL VISION

The Channel Tunnel claims to be the monument
To transport, commerce and the engineering art,
But the lovely downlands have been sadly rent.
With savage wounds, tearing out its very heart.
Soon cars, carriages, lorries, carrying export goods,
Will flood down the myriad railway tracks and roads.
Convoys, blasting, vibrating, through the meadows, woods
With stinking, noisy, dirty and dangerous loads.
Oh Kent, the fair, fruitful garden of England,
Will soon be buried in soulless concrete?
Factories and offices, covering the lush land,
Where once the sky and green hills did meet?
Oh generation that ignores the beauties of creation
With mindless tunnel vision of thoughtless destruction.

Folkestone, July 1991

PROGRESS

Drove once to Folkestone, passage of delight,
The verdant downland welcomed us in.
The tree lined crests, birds in their flight,
Tranquil, restoring after London's din.
Passed into the sweet paradise of Alkham's vale,
Rolling wooded hills, the meadows and pastures green
The fruit farms, wheat fields of that lovely dale
And among the golden corn, the scarlet poppies sheen.
Now brutal, ugly, concrete structures spread,
Interlaced by deep scars where rail and road
Will blight this beauteous place instead,
What for Kent's fair garden, does the future bode?
More frenzy, traffic, pollution for the coming generation,
They call it progress, this barbaric act of desecration.

Folkestone, May 1991

ARMS TRADE SECRECY

What wickedness these arms to sell
Only to create another living hell.
Often to people deprived in every way
Whose subsistence runs from day to day,
Who yearn for freedom, bread and education
But are fed by us with weapons of damnation.
Yet in our land where one third of industry,
Was left to rot under conservative ideology,
The arms trade was fostered by the Thatcher crew,
Against the people's will, connived at by a few.
Secrecy and Governmental check on information
Perverts true Democracy throughout this nation.
So almost on the eve of the Gulf War
Saddam got arms through the back door.
The Thatcher family did well from the odd Arab sheikh:
Mark a million from the sale of tanks did easily rake.
Our mainly Tory press was silent on this score
For lurking just below the surface there was more.
This evil trade the world should now control
Which sadly in our land has assumed a central role.
So tear away the darkness from our public life
Try with sincerity to stem the global strife,
Changing society, business and government,
Seeking ways to live by Christ's covenant.
Where avarice, lying and selfishness are all seen as sin
And where love of God and man alone can bring the Kingdom in.

November 1992

THE BRITISH MUSEUM

The Grecian grace of your majestic portico
Is the gateway to the treasures of antiquity,
Recording older cultures' ebb and flow –
Etruscan, Roman, Saxon, in infamy or glory,
Hellenic balance of body, spirit, mind
Samian ware, sculptures in mysterious harmony.
Here Pharoahs, Buddhas, bearded Assyrians we find,
Artefacts from Asia, of subtle intricacy.
Then the great circular reading room of fame
Where scholars worked in triumph or in vain,
The illuminated codex before the printer came
Inscribing great literature, sacred or profane.
Your lofty tranquil galleries, house great civilisations past
Alas, with our selfish, greedy, modern ways, we may be the last.

Folkestone, November 1992

THE MINERS

They're closing the mines with sinister speed,
Regardless of humanity or the nation's future need.
All part of the dogma of thirteen years past
To swell the three million unemployed forecast.
Our modern, technological society is ruled
By privileged donkeys in science unschooled.
For no future integrated energy policy
Is proposed by this amateur, bungling party.
Our public utilities sold off for a song
Were seen to be going disastrously wrong
As our bills soon soared right up to the skies
To the ripped-off sound of the consumers' cries.
These avaricious new private monopolies
Fuelled by the lust of conservative policies,
Which ruled this land for over thirteen years,
Bringing industrial destruction and economic fears.

Our overseas debt that now stands at over 12 billion pounds
Will be increased by coal imports on lunatic economic grounds.
Monopolies, low investment and corporate fraud,
Insider trading, poor training, friends on the board
Led directly to the Black Wednesday debacle,
That humiliating and shameful national spectacle.
Now the electricity companies purchase gas shares
Rigging the market to price fix their future wares.

The miners must go, they get in the way
Of profitability, the Tories all say.
Short-term policies promoted, regardless of cost

Resources that to future generations will be lost
Showing the face of ruthlessness and greed
Thoughtless of the whole nation's need.
Now closing down the mines with such unseemly haste
With all its consequences in resource and human waste.
We must make sure that at the next election time
We reject the perpetrators of this vicious crime.

Folkestone, October 1992

FOLKESTONE ON REMEMBRANCE SUNDAY

With memory and pride they stand upright,
Chilled in the November wind at the war memorial.
Bright their campaign ribbons in the winter light,
As prayers and hymns are intoned, muted and martial
Accompanied by the soft brass of the Sally Army band.
Meanwhile the ageing veterans in the ranks stand fast
All in the sight of the narrow sea and meagre strand,
Where so many crossed over to the wars of recent past.
Are they musing about the desperate days of battle?
What passes through the grey heads still bravely erect?
Sickness, comradeship, humour or slaughter like cattle?
Or why was I left alive, unworthy here among the elect?
The Last Post poignant floats across the Leas and sea –
Yes, we will remember them praying war will cease to be.

November 1993

REFLECTIONS ON THE DEATH OF PRINCESS DIANA

Great wealth and rank may have their limitation
If your parents part with bitter altercation.
Perhaps the money helps in some small measure,
But the scars of discord can sometimes last forever.
The fairy-tale romance of the Prince and Princess
Was sadly sundered for reasons we can only guess.
The venal media focussed, as rarely seen before,
Upon these personal wounds, so intimate and raw.
They were photographed and filmed around the clock,
With furtive cunning alternately to praise or mock.
To feed the tabloids that so many millions take,
Exploiting the trivial mind with many a lie or fake.
Manipulative power, so difficult to take or check
Chances to be truthful and opportunity also to wreck.

Despite all this, Diana's inner glow came through the hype
With charisma, warmth, style and qualities so hard to type.
Many sought vicariously to share this glamorous domain,
Those with small hope of power or fulfilment to attain.
In thousands they mourned by flower-strewn Palace gate,
The media still active but in a doubtful, contrite state.
Was it sincerity, fantasy or some media-induced mass empathy?
For after years of selfishness and insecurity, came a new unity.
God truly moves in His own mysterious way
Which brought so many people out to mourn and pray.
So may hope, zest, goodness, beauty, joy and loving care
Be an inheritance that, with her sons, we all can share.

September 1997

GERIATRICS

We sometimes say if sex, sport, good food, books
And memory were lost, we should not wish to live,
But in wards and homes they sit and lie,
With vacant faces, unseeing eyes, unhearing ears,
Most of the senses unreceptive to the present world.
Others exist with limbs and speech stroke-frozen,
Often TV roars and flashes with trivia and banality
Lost on them, or maybe bringing other buried images.
Some bare their legs, others sit silent, withdrawn,
In the wards they lie in their own lost worlds,
For the few normal, how many will remain that way?
Some catheterised or with barely-controlled bowels.
Surely this is a kind of half-lived purgatory?
With the quality of life set at almost zero,
Too many old people, too much medical technology?
The guilt and strain on caring families is so evident.
Few seem to become wise, venerable or tranquil in age.
Oh stoic Roman what would you have done?
Fallen on your sword, opened your veins in the bath?
Longevity has a price with so many of the elderly
And making a painless exit is not an option
Within the framework of our present culture.
But who knows what any life is worth?
Except the Almighty.

May 1998

UPON WESTMINTER BRIDGE

"Earth has not anything to show more fair";
But not in 2001's London, I do declare.
A sight so stressful in its urban madness
With traffic noise, fumes, anxiety and stress.

The morning air already toxic, stale
And no sign of merchant ship or sail.
Sunlight filtering through polluted skies.
Smells of onions, burgers and French fries.

Raucous music from open shops and bars
And from some of the myriad passing cars
Never saw I, never felt, alienation so deep
From a city that now never seems to sleep.

The dark polluted river swirls upon its way
Past high buildings that nearly block the day.
Dear God, how could we exclude nature's beauty from our life
Living in ugly, crowded cities that can only bring us strife.

Summer 2001

EDUCATION

Lord, bring to all our teachers courage and inspiration,
Strength for days of stress and times of frustration,
Trying to repair the problems arising from decades of neglect
By elite politicians, whose indifference it does now reflect.
Schools that ought to bring riches of mind and spirit by education
Into the minds of all children requiring confidence and information.
Sadly some will come from homes deprived of wealth, love or instruction,
With missing parent or families that seem doomed to self-destruction.

In a society brainwashed by greed, baseness and triviality
Where commerce dominates culture, fashion and often personality,
And consumerism consumes, for some their very soul,
Manipulated by the TV ads, and tabloids as their goal.
Against these dark forces and the damaged home, we ask
Our teachers to perform their difficult but vital task
Of educating each individual, of class, age, ability or race,
Enriching everyone, and bringing to society, harmony andgrace.

For when we stop learning, we may stop our creative living
And when young, the knowledge spark requires some special giving.
Our teachers then, by Christ's word, have a sacred ministry to pursue,
Knowledge, not only of worldly things but also of the Son and You.
Teaching the need to know your love and to love all your creation,
Bringing the kind of learning that will serve this and every nation.
So Lord be with all teachers who toil by day and often night
To bring wisdom, goodness and beauty into all people's sight.

4th June2001

11 SEPTEMBER 2001

Two silvered planes against a surrealist blue sky
Piloted kamikaze-like, condemning thousands to die,
Into the twin towers, symbols of US power and wealth,
Destroying these great skyscrapers almost by stealth,
Cataclysmic, volcanic explosions, hot, burning fuel,
Dooming those on the top floors to perdition most cruel.
Videoing a hideous new sequence in the infamy of terrorism
Killing, maiming and traumatising these victims of fanaticism
Hellish flame, choking smoke, collapsing buildings beyond repair,
Terrified people diving to their death with fear beyond despair.
Apocalyptic scenes of devastation and man's madness made
And entombing many who sought to bring the victims aid.

So for the dead, injured and bereaved of this insane annihilation,
Our prayers must needs ascend in love, hope and caring consolation.
All this catastrophe was on the TV screens for us to see,
Wondering if it was real or just another disaster movie.
Some children believed it was just such a TV show,
But we must accept that the truth they must soon know.
Most countries declared their horror at such an evil act
And indeed most of all humanity did in such a way react.
But what now – mindless vengeance, or some kind of reconciliation?
For in the Gaza streets some danced with joyous jubilation.

The squalid refugee camps of the Middle East have housed
Arabs whose anger and despair much bitter hatred have aroused.
And the poverty and hunger of many Third World nations
Are blamed on the influence of the multinational corporations.
Together with crippling debts and US-influenced trade restrictions.

And now comes an asylum flood, which is sweeping to the west,
It will not be resolved until all these problems are addressed.

So it may not profit to just punish the Afghan state,
When among two billion Moslems there remains such hate.
The Germans were forgiven and aided, despite their great barbarity
And then took their place among the civilised world's family.
Forgiving your enemies can therefore be achieved
And from future violence the whole planet be relieved.
Certainly justice must swiftly follow its course
But the roots of evil must be tackled at their source.
And war against the Islamic world may not be wise
For from the death of innocents, fresh terrorists will arise.
Also the destruction in Manhattan could trigger a market fall,
With a recession and oil crisis wreaking havoc for us all.

So we need then to love, to hope, to think and pray,
Have faith in God and mankind to expunge this evil day.
To learn to love and share the fruits of this creation,
To banish want and ignorance in this and every nation.
Christ's message of service and sacrifice must still be learned
So a new world can arise from ashes of the towers that burned.
Then light and peace can come from the darkness of this terror
And the whole Earth be healed through love's invincible endeavour.

September 2001

A PRAYER FOR NURSES

Lord we pray for nurses here and everywhere
Knowing we entrust our loved ones to their care
The old, and young, middle-aged, those new-born,
The sick, accident victims, those by crime forlorn.
Some who seem hardly living in this day and age,
The blind, deaf, memory lost and mindless rage.
They carefully dress the wounds, rashes, ulcers, sores,
Calming trauma and anxieties and humouring the bores.
Dealing with faeces, wet sheets and vomit every day,
Always, with so little time to stop, to rest and pray.

Nights disturbed by plaintive or shrill cries so tearful,
Stilling the restless, distressed and the many fearful.
Some patients, violent, angry, often much confused,
Sadly some by family maltreated or abused.
Times when the A and E is like some Babel's hell,
With drunks or addicts, sometimes criminals as well.
Nurses must be mindful of diagnoses and treatments,
Be calm, despite haste, fatigue and frequent arguments.

The nurse needs such strength and love for all who call
So may the power of the Holy Spirit be upon them all.
Father, watch over those who tend the sick and lame,
Every day and night, serving patients in Christ's name.

1st February 2004

PEACE

Peace is the fading summer light over sea and hills.
Peace is true wisdom, the creativity of caring wills.
Peace is stillness after passionate nearness.
Peace is love of creation and unselfishness.
Peace lies in curbing ego's calculating or thoughtless course.
Peace lies in resisting dominance by violence, stealth or force.
Peace lies in stemming escapism, excess pleasure, consumerism.
Peace lies in checking power, lust, noise and savage sensualism.
Peace comes with hope to dispel despair.
Peace comes in truths in which we all share.
Peace comes with beauty in creative work and reflection.
Peace is in the still centre of us and the source of all creation.
Peace is goodness which by God's grace we may come to know.
Peace passing all understanding, then into us will flow.

February 1993